LITTLE WHITE BOOK OF

WEDDING PLANNING WISDOM

LITTLE WHITE BOOK OF

WEDDING PLANNING WISDOM

NICOLE FRAIL

Illustrated by Kerri Frail

Skyhorse Publishing

Skyhorse Publishing books may be purchased in bulk at special discounts for sales promotion, corporate gifts, fund-raising, or educational purposes. Special editions can also be created to specifications. For details, contact the Special Sales Department, Skyhorse Publishing, 307 West 36th Street, 11th Floor, New York, NY 10018 or info@skyhorsepublishing.com.

Skyhorse® and Skyhorse Publishing® are registered trademarks of Skyhorse Publishing, Inc.®, a Delaware corporation.

Visit our website at www.skyhorsepublishing.com.

10 9 8 7 6 5 4 3 2 1

Library of Congress Cataloging-in-Publication Data is available on file.

Cover design by Kerri Frail
Cover photo credit ThinkStock/kameshkova and ThinkStock/ OlgaLebedeva

Print ISBN: 978-1-63220-277-2
Ebook ISBN: 978-1-5107-0065-9

Printed in China

To my grandmother, Rachel Nardone, who told my high school boyfriend to propose.

And to Matthew, for eventually doing as he was told.

Contents

Introduction   ix

1. The Engagement   1
2. Get Organized   15
3. Budget with a Capital B   23
4. The Venue Verdict   31
5. Finding the Very Best Vendors   43
6. Dress Shopping   78
7. Wedding Bands   106
8. The Parties—The People and the Places   123
9. The Devil's in the Details   144
10. Your Wedding Day   176

Quotes   191
A Few Links For You   197
Resources   198
Acknowledgments   200
Index   202

Introduction

When I started writing this book, I had never been married nor engaged; however, I knew a proposal was coming, and I had teased Matthew, my then-boyfriend of nine years, that I had two introductions planned: one in which I got to talk about planning my own wedding, and one in which I didn't.

Hint hint.

But he didn't need the hint; he'd already bought the ring. On the last day of summer 2014, he lit every candle we owned, got down on one knee in our living room, and the rest is history.

And so here I am, writing a book about wedding planning as I dive into my own plans. In an effort to be completely honest, I'll let you know that I'm not a wedding planner by trade. However, after writing this book, everything so far has been be a breeze! (Knock on wood.) I've asked all the questions I've told you to ask, I've followed all my own advice, and I'm attempting to go against the grain and tradition as often as I can. Hopefully you and I will get through this together without any disasters or too many tears!

This book is small—too small to contain every little bit of information you'll need while you plan. I haven't included lists of flower types and in which seasons they bloom; I haven't created a complete checklist for your day-of emergency kit; I haven't provided you with every single itty-bitty step of the process. Think of this book as a good starting point, an overview.

If you're the type of bride who simply wants to get some ideas and then take off on her own, this book is for you. If you're the type of person who likes to buck tradition, I have tried my best to give you some alternatives to the expectations that surround the typical wedding. I have also tried to make this book all-inclusive. I want every type of bride marrying the love of her life to be able to use this book. (All bridesmaids, bridesmen, groomsgals, groomsmen, best men, best women, and maids/matrons/men of honor are also welcome to flip through the pages while helping their brides and grooms plan for their big day.)

I am also making the grand assumption that you're reading this book because you're planning your first wedding. However, we all know what happens when we assume . . . and I do hope that if this is your second or third or even fourth celebration, there's still something in here that maybe you didn't think of the first time or a new idea that you can play with and make your own.

As you read, you'll find that I've incorporated a variety of quotes throughout the book. Some are from celebrities or professional wedding/event planners, and others are from men and women like you and me. These former brides and grooms (current husbands and wives) have been through it all and have volunteered, via social media, to help us on our journeys by sharing tips and lessons they learned during their own planning processes.

Whether the advice is on love, marriage, or weddings or comes from Emily Bronte, Vera Wang, Christina M. in Florida, or me, I hope you find it helpful. I hope your wedding planning process is painless, exciting, and fun. And I hope you realize that you really shouldn't sweat the small stuff—if a napkin is folded incorrectly or a centerpiece is off-center, you're most likely going to be the only one who notices. Focus on the big stuff: you're getting married! Enjoy it and everything that comes with it!

Congratulations, and good luck!

1

The Engagement

"Whatever our souls are made of, his and mine are the same."
—EMILY BRONTE

• • •

*F*or one of two reasons, you picked up this book: 1) you're engaged (and, if so, a heartfelt congratulations to you is in order) or 2) you know someone who is (and you've been suckered into helping them plan the wedding-to-be).

Let's assume for this chapter that you have a new ring on your finger and you're dying to tell everyone about it and get the party (literally) started!

But before you book your dream venue, start arguments over napkin folding, and drag your fiancé or maid of honor all over town to listen to every local band known to man, let's just take a deep breath and . . .

Enjoy the moment!

I realize that in today's technological world, you have the ability to take a photo and upload it for the world to see while your guy or girl is still on one knee, but . . . that doesn't mean you have to. If that's going to make both of you happy, then go for it—post the photo, blog about the proposal, hashtag the hell out of every status you post for the next week.

However, many wedding resources stress the importance of taking the time to reflect on what's happened before you share your big news with the world. I'm not telling you to rethink your acceptance of the proposal (although, you definitely want to make sure this is what you want before you say yes!), but spending a few hours (or even days, if you're so inclined) with your fiancé dreaming up your perfect future and wondering who to share the news with first—and how—may be a good idea.

Remember, you're getting married because you want to spend the rest of your lives together. You value the idea, practice,

and act of marriage, and you want to show *each other* how much you love, respect, and honor one another other. You don't need to prove your commitment or love to anyone else.

How to Break the News

After reality has sunk in, it's time to share your news with those closest to you—unless you've already posted a zillion pictures on Instagram, Twitter, and Facebook and have pinned your dream dress on Pinterest. In that case, everyone closest to you *and* those random "friends" you accepted because they seem interesting. And that person you haven't spoken to since kindergarten? They already know.

If you haven't documented your engagement online, take a more personal approach and call, Skype, or visit the people most important to you and who you feel will be the most supportive throughout the next several months or years. These may be family members—parents, grandparents, siblings, cousins—or best friends, neighbors, coworkers . . . anyone you think will be excited for the step you're taking and who may be involved in the process.

Who'd You Tell First?

"I immediately called my mom. . . . I think his parents already knew, and my parents already knew because he asked my dad permission first. I think he called his family the next day to tell them I said yes." —ARDI A.

"Parents first, then everyone else. In person for close parents, and phone for far away parents. That's how it was for us." —MARIE J.

"My parents were away when he proposed, so the first people I told were my friends, another couple we had over for dinner." —BERNADETTE F.

"We were at the beach for the weekend. It was like 11:30 p.m. and I called my mom bawling my eyes out. When I kept trying to say John proposed, I couldn't get the words out and she thought something happened to John. She was like, 'Lindsay, calm down! Where's John!?' We called his parents the next day because they go to bed early." —LINDSAY S.

"No one in my family knew my fiancé was going to propose except my parents since he called the night before for permission. When we agreed to have thoughtful gifts on Christmas related to both being in school, we decided on poems to each other. The way he gathered my family's attention before reading his poem got me suspicious. About halfway through the poem, my brother-in-law began recording the event on his phone including his kneel, my reaction, and the numerous vocal reactions of my family watching. We told my brother and his wife out of state by sending the video via text message; it was a wonderful way to include them in the special moment and tell the good news." —STACE K.

Once all the "important" people find out, then you should go crazy. Post the photos, write the blogs, hashtag your heart out. Just make sure your significant other is comfortable with all the attention, both online and off.

What about engagement photos and announcements?

Some couples (see also: some couples' parents and grandparents) have always imagined that once this moment happened, they'd flipped through their local newspaper and see their smiling faces in print in the Weddings section. While this isn't something *everyone* is doing these days, it could be a cute idea and makes a great keepsake if you're a scrapbooker.

Regardless of whether that announcement is something you desire, you're most likely considering the option of hiring a professional photographer to take engagement photographs to commemorate the occasion, use to build websites, stuff in wedding invites, and enlarge for your upcoming celebrations. If you've always secretly wanted to model, you have the money, and your fiancé supports the idea, then put some feelers out and find yourself a worthy photog. Just be sure you get your money's worth—you want outfit changes, different venues/scenery, good lighting, the ability to reschedule if the weather is horrid, and a professional experience (give or take a variety of animals—my research turned up an engagement photo of a couple with a horse and a dog in the picture). Don't hire the first person who promises to

put you in front of a tree, hand you a hat, and tell you to smile wide. And don't feel obligated to hire your fiancé's sister's son, who took a photography class in high school and sometimes still snaps photos with the lens on. Just because he dreams of working for *National Geographic* doesn't mean he's the right person to shoot these once-in-a-lifetime photos.

(Remember these things when you're booking a wedding photographer, too! For more information on this part, see page 47.)

Once you have photographs you're happy with, you can submit them to your hometown newspaper, college alumni magazines and newsletters, and even post them online—as long as you sign a release with the photographer. Technically, they own the rights to those photographs (they created them; you're simply in them), so be sure they're okay with you posting them on your personalized pages from sites such as OurWeddingDay. com or TheKnot.com.

Unless you're having a short engagement, you can hold off on the formal Save the Dates at this point. The time to send those, as we'll discuss later, is about one year before the actual date of the wedding.

Why isn't she happy for me?

I wanted to take an honest approach to this book, so, here it is: it's no secret women get jealous. And sometimes that jealousy gets in the way of their support, excitement, and genuine happiness when their girlfriends are engaged. Sure, men can be taken by a bit of envy from time to time, but for the most part, ladies, this issue is typically one that involves us.

So why is she not exactly thrilled? Maybe she's been dating the same guy for almost ten years and he's taking his sweet time with his proposal. Maybe she's recently had a relationship fall through and she's still hurting. Maybe she's your older sister or cousin and she thought she'd be the first girl in the family to get married. Or maybe you've been best friends since grade school and news of your engagement has her worried that she's losing you.

Either way, give her some time to get used to the idea and to see that, with or without her enthusiasm, it's happening. In a few weeks, ask her to get drinks or coffee with you and talk it out, if possible.

Oh, and if she's one of the women you were thinking of asking to be part of the wedding party, hold off for a little while just to make sure it's a good match. She'll probably come around, but if she doesn't, you'll regret that negative energy stinking up the place on your big day.

What if our families don't know each other?

Though nearly 50 percent of all couples cohabitate before they get engaged or married, many of these couples' parents have not yet met. If the couple—cohabitating or not—lives away from one or both sets of parents, it may be more than a little difficult to bring everyone together for holidays and special occasions—such as the celebration or announcement of your engagement.

If they haven't met and they don't live close enough to meet, one set should call the other. Traditionally, the groom's parents would call the bride's to show that they're welcoming the bride into their family; however, traditions are broken and revamped every day, so it doesn't matter who makes the call, so long as it's made within two or three days of the announcement. Otherwise, one (or both) sets of parents may wonder if the other doesn't agree with the marriage.

If your parents have never met but they'd like to and you have room to spare, you can plan a small get-together at your place—neutral territory—and ask them both to come meet in person shortly after you've shared the news of your engagement. If this isn't possible, you can always wait until the engagement party, should you decide to have one, to introduce both sides of the family to one another.

Regardless of when it happens, just be sure that it does in fact happen. If both sides, specifically both sets of parents, are familiar with one another, the planning will be much smoother going forward.

FAQs—The Ones *They'll* Be Asking *You*

Although you'll be doing your fair share of questioning in the coming months, you'll also be the ones providing many (many) answers to those flung at you by friends, family, coworkers, and even strangers as early as the second you announce your engagement. These may include:

- Have you set a date yet?

- What colors have you chosen? What's the theme?
- Who's in the wedding party? Who's the maid of honor/best man?
- Where are you saying your vows? Are you writing your own?
- How did (name) react to the news? Are you inviting him/her?
- Are you getting married in the church? What will Grandpa say if you don't?
- Are you/your partner pregnant?

Regardless of the question, do *not* feel that you need to provide the answer. Maybe it's early in your engagement and you don't have them yet, or maybe you don't feel comfortable sharing them with whoever asked the question. It's okay to say, "Oh, I'm not sure yet," smile, and change the subject or pretend to get a phone call.

Throwing an Engagement Party

Let's get one thing straight: you *don't* need to have an engagement party if you don't want one—just like you don't need to wear heels, your bridesmaid dresses don't need to match, and you don't need to invite your Uncle Benny's third cousin's kid to your wedding if you don't want to. It's very important that, from the very beginning, it's *your* day. Don't fall victim to other people's expectations, suggestions, and even demands.

Traditionally, someone else hosts and plans the engagement party or engagement dinner. Sometimes it's the bride's

Did you have an engagement party?

"We didn't have an engagement party; life is just too hectic!" —CRYSTAL H.

"Carl and I had a party. At the time, we liked to have parties. It was pretty low key. We invited everyone who was invited to the wedding. . . . Someone threw it for me but I was right in there helping. Like I said, it wasn't too formal." —MARIE J.

"I didn't really care to have one; we were more focused on starting to plan the wedding." —KATE R.

"No engagement party for me. It was the holiday season so we were already out visiting family. Too much stress to have to plan a big event." —STACE K.

"My dear pal, Jayne, threw a surprise engagement/going away party for Dave and me; we were moving from Virginia to Louisiana at the time." —FILOMENA N.

"No engagement party for me. My mother yelled at my fiancé because we were already living together. She told him he should have proposed before I moved in with him. It was the eighties." —GLORIA B.

parents, sometimes it's the groom's . . . sometimes it's a friend of the family or your best man/maid of honor, if you've already asked him/her to take on that role. These are usually smaller affairs—oftentimes a cocktail hour followed by a nice dinner—though it could be more of a barbeque or even a weekend getaway.

The party or dinner typically takes place two to three months after the engagement. It *shouldn't* take place within six months of the actual wedding, as many other events happening in the weeks leading up to your wedding will take up much of your time. Having an engagement party in the midst of all that will drive everyone crazy.

Who is invited to the celebration should not be up to only the host of the party or dinner; they should consult you before the final invites—whether hardcopy or electronic—are sent. It should go without saying that if you don't plan on inviting certain people to your wedding, then they shouldn't receive an invite to the engagement party.

One more point to make before we move on: guests are not expected to bring gifts to the engagement party. If they do, thank them and put the gift to the side until the end of the night; don't open the gift in front of your other attendees. Privately thank the gift-giver in a letter, email, or over the phone the next day, but don't make any announcements during the dinner or party thanking those who did give.

Is this a team effort, or are you flying solo?

Once the excitement is down to a dull roar and the news is (somewhat) old, it's time to have a very important conversation with your partner. Though you may have already agreed on and announced a few details that you discussed pre-engagement (date, wedding party, colors, venue), the majority of the hardcore planning has not yet taken place. It's vital you sit down with your partner and decide how involved each of you will be from this point forward.

Ideally, both partners will participate equally. If this is the case, start by making a tentative list of all the things that probably need to be done and assign tasks to each of you that you're individually most interested in. Maybe you'll want to do some (or all) things together; make a note of that, too. Then hang the list somewhere you'll both see it—don't put it in a binder that you can both pile your crap on when you get home from work and you're tired and grumpy. Hang the list on the fridge, on the front door, on a bulletin board—somewhere at eye level that you can't miss. Recognize the list is a priority; if these things don't get done, you'll both be panicked, anxious, and miserable the closer you get to the big day.

At this time, you also need to agree on who gets the final say on any decisions involving multiple parties. If your partner's parents are paying for the flowers, then do they get to choose the flowers or do you? If your father's paying for the rehearsal dinner, then does he get to say where it will be or will you? If you're planning the wedding on your own and your partner is supporting this, then does that mean he or she doesn't want to be consulted on lighting, chair covers, the cake, or music? Figure this out now to avoid issues in the future.

One last thing to consider, whether you're planning this wedding on your own, together, or with a planner: the two of you should *always* appear to be on the same page. You should

If you're doing all the work, is there anything he can do?

Many grooms like to sit on the sidelines while their brides run around smelling flower after flower and spend their weekends making party favors. If that's how the bride wants it to be, that's perfectly fine. However, if the bride wants to talk about all the work she's doing, then she should be able to do so. This is where the groom can finally pitch in: he can listen.

Let her vent about cousin Kristy, who is "busy" every time she tries to get the bridesmaids together, or the wedding planner, who just can't seem to comprehend which shade of blue she really wants the tablecloths to be. Let her get it all out, pour her a glass of wine, offer to rub her shoulders . . . do *something*. After all, you already don't have much to do!

appear united. You should not agree to something without the other present. If your mother tries to get you to choose a cake flavor the weekend your partner is away on business, tell her you need to wait to make the decision. If his sister desperately wants the centerpieces to be four feet tall and you're not part of the discussion, then he needs to tell her that they can revisit the topic the next time you're present. This shows that you respect each other and that you will not let anyone else take over the planning of a day that is rightfully *yours*.

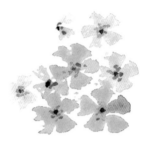

2

Get Organized

"Marriage is not the beginning of the journey, nor the end—it is the journey." —CAREW PAPRITZ, *The Legacy Letters: His Wife, His Children, His Final Gift*

So, you've been engaged for a few weeks (or months, if you've decided to have a longer engagement) and you've stopped staring dreamily at your pretty new piece of jewelry long enough to get back to your everyday life. Everyone who needs to know about your engagement does, and things have generally calmed down.

Every couple has a different approach to how they move forward from this point. Some brides and grooms to-be are ready to jump in to the planning process *right this second*. The day your partner popped the question, you may have chosen the date, decided who would be in the wedding party, and even announced where you hoped to have your reception. The very next day, Mom may have subscribed you to magazines like *Martha Stewart Weddings* and *Bridal Guide* and you may have penciled a tentative seating chart on a napkin while out for coffee with your best friend. While all of this is fine (and comes with the territory of being excited!), simply verbalizing what you want and skipping from subject to subject with different people, and without actually making any concrete plans, can get frustrating.

For most of us, this is why now is *not* the time to start planning the wedding. Instead, it's the time to *get ready to start* planning. This is when you figure out what you will need to do as the day approaches; it's not the time to start checking off everything on the list.

This chapter may be something a compulsive list-maker or post-it note perfectionist may want to skip. For those of you who "forget" to make the bed in the morning, eat dinner on your couch because the table is too cluttered, or can't see the top of your desk at work, then my goal is to try to help you get to a place that will make the actual planning of the wedding a bit easier. My goal is to help you get organized.

Note: You may also want to skip this chapter if you're having a short engagement and you actually do need to dive right into things. If that's the case, see chapter 3 for budgets, chapter 4 for venues, and chapter 5 for vendors.

Start with the Space

By *space*, I don't mean the venue where you want to have your ceremony or reception. This time, we're talking about the area of your apartment, house, or bedroom where you're going to store everything wedding-related that you gather along this process. This may all be common sense, but sometimes it helps to see things on paper, so I'll spell it out for you anyway.

Pick a place that is accessible to you and your partner, so he or she may add anything they find or want to discuss. I recommend you clear a shelf for all your magazines, books, binders, and notebooks. This way, the spines will face out and you'll be able to easily locate exactly what you need in a pinch. Displaying your materials like this will be easier than having to route through a pile in the corner, dig inside a box labeled WEDDING SH!T, or clear off your kitchen or coffee table every time you have guests over for a non-wedding-related discussion. (Though few and far between, those should still occur during this time in your life!)

For anything that may not fit snuggly on a shelf, then you can start a box and place it somewhere near the shelf, if possible. These items may include sample centerpieces, bridesmaid gifts, parts of any DIY projects, etc. When one box gets three-quarters of the way full, don't try to cram more in it, as you may damage what's already inside. To ensure you know what's inside each box, label them. Add items to the label as you add them to the box.

Once you have a set space for everything you'll inevitably accumulate while you plan your wedding, you will then have to decide what needs to be the most accessible. As discussed in chapter 1, making lists of things you need to eventually do is an obvious part of wedding planning. If items or actions on the list are urgent, however, then you may want to place the list somewhere both of you will see it—on the fridge, the inside of the front door, the bedroom or bathroom mirror.

Things to Do Now

Although the majority of your planning can happen later, there are a few things that, if decided right now, would make the rest of the process easier. In fact, some of these things do need to be decided before you can actually move ahead. The following do not need to be done in the order listed (you may need to know your budget before you set the date, for example).

Agree on Your Budget

The most important decision you can make before jumping into full-on wedding planning is how much money you're going to be able to spend on it—and where you're going to get it. Who will be helping pay? Your parents? Your spouse's? Will you be handling it on your own? Will you put it all on credit? Can you afford a wedding planner? Save the dates *and* official invitations? A ceremony dress and a party dress?

Budget's a big deal, and you both need to be on the same page before you spend a single cent. To find out a bit more about budgeting for your big day, see chapter 3.

Set a Date

For some, setting a date may be simple; perhaps you always had a date in mind—an anniversary of a special day, a loved one's birthday you'd like to honor, or maybe you always wanted a White Wedding with snow and icicle lights on Christmas weekend. I've heard one story in which the bride-to-be wanted to get married on a certain date, but wanted it to fall on a specific day of the week, so the couple was engaged several years before that date and that weekday arrived.

If you know exactly what day you want and you won't take no for an answer, then congrats! Your job here is done. Time to move on!

However, for most couples, choosing a date isn't that easy. Maybe the bride has a dream venue rather than a dream date in mind, and she'll have to wait until the venue is available. Maybe the budget that has been set won't accommodate an October or November wedding, but March and April is do-able. Maybe your religion won't allow weddings on specific days, or your family has a reunion or another big event planned that won't allow half the guest list to RSVP yes to your celebration.

Pick the month that seems to work best for you and then consider each week in that month. Does your company have a retreat planned? Does your sister *hate* sharing her birthday with anything or anyone? Are your parents planning a getaway? Don't forget to look out for national events, too. Consider airfare and hotel fees for out-of-town attendees on holiday weekends. In April, for example, *The Knot* suggests you don't plan your wedding the weekend before tax day. People are stressed by the looming deadline, may not be able to afford a wedding gift or

Things to Consider When Choosing a Wedding Date

The season matters. If it's too hot outside, tempers may flare along with the sun.

Some months are more expensive than others. Wedding sources agree that peak wedding months are May through September because, depending on the region, these months will offer the best weather for the occasion. The charge from the wedding site won't be the highest one you'll see during this time; every vendor, florist, caterer, and hotel will jack up prices during these months.

As are time periods. A daytime wedding will cost significantly less—sometimes $100 per person less—than a nighttime event. Nighttime weddings also tend to be more formal, requiring you and your guests to spend a bit more on attire and accessories to fit the part.

And some days are, too. Friday and Saturday nights cost more than Sundays. And weekdays, though difficult to fit into all attendees' schedules, are the cheapest of all. Hotel rates for your guests will also be more expensive on weekends and during the holiday season.

transport to the wedding, and accountants and tax lawyers may need to skip the event altogether!

Just be sure that once you set your date, you don't let anyone change your mind. You chose your date for a reason; don't let

Great Aunt Mina's superstitions or your best friend's boyfriend's yet-to-be-planned bros-only camping trip change your mind.

Choose a Religion—or Don't

Is it important for you and your partner to incorporate any religious or spiritual aspects into your wedding ceremony? Or are you going to take a non-religious or civil/secular approach? Decide this now; discuss how many Christian, Jewish, Islam, Hindu, etc. traditions you'd like to uphold. Do you want to honor one or more?

Before you start planning, you should have all of these details ironed out, as your venue—or at least your ceremony space—and officiant may depend on your religious requirements.

Tip!

Set up an email account for all the wedding sites, contests, giveaways, etc. that you're bound to find online. One leads to another and before you know it, you'll be inundated with chances to win free dresses, honeymoons, and favors. If it helps, you could also use this email for RSVPs.

Things to Do Later

You'll be thinking about plenty of things during this time period, but many of them—especially if your wedding is still a year or more away—can be put off. However, if you have ideas, there's no reason you can't write them down. You may find yourself making notes to refer to later regarding:

- **Wedding Party**—Who will be your maid/matron of honor and bridesmaids? Best man and groomsmen? Ushers? Will your wedding parties be mixed-gendered?
- **Theme/Style**—Do you like navy blue or Carolina blue? Is red an okay color for a summer wedding, or should you go with blush? Do you really like the nautical theme *that* much?
- **Favors**—What do you want to give your guests to remember your day? Magnets? Champagne flutes? Candy bars with your faces on them?
- **Guest List**—Who are you *definitely* inviting? Who are the maybes? If Frank invited you to his wedding, but you didn't go, do you need to invite him to yours?
- **Reception Entertainment**—Live music, DJ, or a little of both? Photo booth or disposable cameras on all the tables? Will there be an after-party?
- **Dress Shopping**—Where will you go? Who will go with you? What style is best for your body?

3

Budget with a Capital B

"I discovered I'm actually planning two weddings—the one
inspired by Pinterest and the one I can actually afford."*

*B*efore you can finalize anything—your venue, your guest
list, your dress, your centerpieces—you need to know what
you're working with; you need to know your maximum budget.
I promise you, coming up with this number won't be the most
fun you'll have during the process, but it's definitely the most
important factor and it will allow you to move on to the other
stuff—the stuff you actually want to talk about and focus on.

The first thing you need to know is who will be paying for
all expenses: you and your partner? Just your partner? Your
partner's father? Your grandmother? Will you be splitting costs?
And if so, fifty-fifty? Sixty-forty?

In some cases, you may already have part of this answer—
maybe your mother always told you that she had a wedding fund

---

* SomeEcards.com / delightful crab.

put away for your big day or maybe your fiancé's parents told him how much they could contribute when he told them he'd proposed.

Once you know where the outside finances are coming from, sit down with your soon-to-be spouse and figure out how much the two of you can put into the celebration.

As of this writing, the average cost of a wedding in the United States is $25,000—before honeymoon. Though many couples can hold their wedding ceremonies for less than $10,000, the average couple will spend between $18,900 and $31,500.

However, just because *other* couples are spending these amounts doesn't mean that you have to. If your cousin's wedding cost her $40,000, there's no reason you need to try to match that. If you have $5,000 to spend, then you have $5,000 to spend—do *not* go over your max budget or you won't be able to enjoy your honeymoon or, in some cases, your first year (or longer) of marriage!

Not to bring anyone down, but in 2014, a study performed by Andrew M. Francis and Hugo M. Mialon and published as "'A Diamond is Forever' and Other Fairy Tales: The Relationship between Wedding Expenses and Marriage Duration" found that

couples who spent more than $20,000 on their weddings were 3.5 times more likely to divorce than those who spent between $5,000 and $10,000. Something to keep in mind . . .

Priorities

Before you start your research into particular venues, caterers, or transportation services, be sure you know which aspects of the wedding are most important to you. Would you choose flowers over Save the Dates? If the reception is being held at night, should you spend more money on lighting or transportation? Will your guests have a better time on the dance floor or in the dessert line? Are you willing to spend an extra 40 percent on an experienced, professional photographer or will your little sister's Nikon do the job? What do you want people to take away from your special day?

Once you've set your priorities—those things that you absolutely *must* have at your ceremony or reception—then designate an approximate amount of money for each. Of the aforementioned $25,000 spent on weddings in the United States, the Wedding Report estimates the following is spent by the average couple:

- $11,000 on venue, catering, and rentals
- $4,000 on jewelry
- $2,600 on photography
- $1,600 on attire and accessories
- $1,500 on flowers and decorations
- $1,200 on entertainment

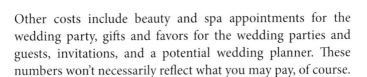

Other costs include beauty and spa appointments for the wedding party, gifts and favors for the wedding parties and guests, invitations, and a potential wedding planner. These numbers won't necessarily reflect what you may pay, of course.

What did you budget the most money for?

"Reception and food! My biggest waste in money was on flowers, though. They all look pretty, but they die by the end of the day and no one remembers them. The most important things were definitely food and music because people want to be satisfied with their meal and remember they had a good time!" —LINDSAY S.

"We spent the most on the food/reception venue. Our friends are party animals so it was really important to us to have an open bar, but it certainly cost us! I wouldn't change that choice for the world though; we had the best party!" —JEN B.

"I splurged on a great photographer because the pictures last forever." —@LALUPUSLADY

"Photography. The pictures will be all you have left when it's over. And veils, of course." —@JULIA_BELLES

"The reception as a whole—food, drink, entertainment. We wanted a fun party." —JESS L.

"I spent the most on flowers. I sewed my own wedding dress and baked all the breads and the cake (my maid of honor decorated the cake); my friends helped us chop up the vegetables and cheeses; and my brother-in-law's band provided the music. I love roses, though, and I knew our wedding was my big chance to surround myself with them." —SARAH C.

Do Not Sacrifice What Will Make You Happy

It's really important to keep in mind that this is, once again, *your* day. Though you want your friends and family to take away fun and happy memories of their own, this is your one and only wedding and you need to make sure it's everything you want it to be. While you're determining your priorities, make sure you're not self-sacrificing. If you feel strongly that you want Save the Dates, but your mother doesn't think it's worth the money, stand your ground. If you've decided that good photographs are the only things that matter and you want to budget more money for photos than for food or entertainment, then make sure your partner knows that and is on your side. If you are very strongly against consuming alcohol and you would have a rotten time if everyone was drunk around you at your reception, then have a dry wedding or don't have an open bar. This is about you and your partner, and everyone else's opinions should take the back seat.

What Do You Already Have Lined Up?

Again, before spending money, evaluate what you're already saving money on and don't list those as expenses: If you're getting married on your family's property, lake-side, then what other couples might spend on their venues might be able to go toward food or entertainment. If your uncle owns a limo company and has volunteered to drive your wedding party and guests from ceremony to reception, then you can perhaps spend a few more dollars on your dream dress. If your brother is in a band and offers to play at your reception as a gift to you— and you like the band's music—then maybe you can afford an open bar.

Stay Organized

Once you have a max budget in place and you know approximately which percentages of your budget will go where, create a spreadsheet or make an easy-to-follow table in a notebook you'll be able to easily find. Share the spreadsheet with your partner and—if they've requested to be kept in the loop—anyone contributing money to your big day.

Every time you write a check, sign a contract, or receive some type of verbal or written (always try to get written!) confirmation, mark it down with the date—just in case.

Once you know what you're working with and who is helping you, you can move on to the fun stuff!

Is a Wedding Planner Necessary?

The simple answer here is no, hiring a wedding planner is not something you *must* do—especially if you're taking a very do-it-yourself approach to your nuptials. If your bridal party is willing to help, if your mother wants to be involved, or if your maid of honor knows her away around a wedding binder like the back of her hand, you may not need a professional. However, if you're going at it alone, are too busy with work and life to plan, or you'd just feel more comfortable with the help, then be sure to consider this cost when setting your budget.

But is it ever too early to contact a wedding planner?

Katherine Cassell, an event planner based in New York City, says no. "There is no need to rush; it is a good idea to take the time to search around and perhaps meet with a few different wedding planners before actually booking. However, you definitely want to book early enough so that your wedding planner can secure your date. I wouldn't suggest booking more than sixteen months in advance (unless you are throwing an extravagant, involved wedding). The main reason why I say no is because wedding planners are typically working on multiple events at a time. While the bulk of your wedding work won't happen until the six- to eight-month mark, it is a good idea for your wedding planner to be able to have you on their future radar."

4

The Venue Verdict

"Planning without action is futile;
acting without planning is fatal."
—UNKNOWN

• • •

*M*ost people like to book their venues (ceremony and reception site) a year and a half to a year before their weddings. This will ensure that you have the space you want and have enough time to organize the rest.

Before you make any appointments or start Googling venues, take some time to figure out exactly what you need. If it's a small affair, perhaps a tent or a family member's backyard will do the trick. If you're not planning to have your ceremony in a church, synagogue, or mosque, then perhaps it can be at your reception site. If you've dreamed of an outdoor wedding, but you're planning it during the rainy season, you'll want to be sure the site you choose will accommodate a Plan B.

Size Matters

First, make a tentative guest list. One of the most important things in booking the right venue is making sure that everyone you want to share the day with will be able to attend—comfortably. You don't want any guests to go without a seat during the ceremony or dinner, and the dance floor and cocktail hour space needs to be big enough to have a good time without bumping into one another.

Talk to your partner (and perhaps consult with your mother) about who you definitely want to invite—and don't forget to add your bridal party and yourselves to the final number. Be sure you're on the same page about inviting children, plus-ones for certain guests, and friends of friends or second or third cousins. Be sure to also note which tentative guests you'd be okay *not* inviting if you had to cut a few to fit venue requirements.

Remember, again, that this day is about *both of you*. If you want to invite someone whose presence will upset or anger your bride/groom, then think hard about doing so. If your partner is unhappy on your wedding day, won't you be, too? This is the perfect time to practice your communication skills—talk with each other and make the decision that's best for both of you.

And if it comes down to it, remember these wise words from my mother: "If you don't want to be invited to their wedding, don't invite them to yours."

Your Style

Once you have a tentative number, you should examine the notes you've been taking (and pins you've been pinning, photos

> **Tip!**
>
> This is *not* the time to start gathering addresses (or email addresses) of friends and family you plan on inviting. Since you haven't yet finalized the list, you don't want to ask for an address only to later discover that you can't invite that person due to space/budget limitations. All you need right now are the names. Don't set yourself up for guilt or an awkward conversation later.

you've been saving, and links you've been sharing) about your sense of style. Have you decided on a theme? Colors? Flowers? Do you know if you prefer a certain type of lighting or floor? Perhaps your wedding will be in the fall and you've decided that you want to bring some of the outdoors in.

There are millions of options when it comes to styling your wedding—and hundreds of books you could read to tell you how to do so. Whatever you decide as a couple, just make sure you take notes as you go and that you're both on the same page when it comes time to share your thoughts and ideas with others.

When the time comes to meet with representatives or planners from ceremony or reception sites, be clear about what you're envisioning. Bring examples—photos of other weddings, pages from magazines, swatch colors, etc.—to your meetings and show them what you're referring to.

Remember three important things about working your personal style into your big day:

1. **You don't need to pick just one**—theme, color, flower, etc. Your pre-wedding events do not have to match your wedding.

2. **Don't accept no for an answer**—these coordinators do this for a living and they should know how to work with you to make this the day you want it to be. Don't allow them to make decisions for you and don't let them shut down your ideas. Ask them to collaborate with you, and if you can't get along, don't work with them at all.

3. **Be flexible**—sometimes the budget, space, or people involved just won't work out. Try not to get too attached to an idea, a certain shade of pink, or a particular menu item. If it doesn't work or it can't happen, take a second, accept it, and move on. Don't make yourself and everyone around you miserable by being insistent and aggravating.

What made the venue you booked attractive to you?

"It was more about the feeling than something visible. But the water view helped, too." —JULIE G.

"Our wedding venue offered a lot of food for a good price!" —CRYSTAL S.

"After months spent planning every teeny weeny detail at a do-it-yourself hall, I said screw it, and went to a 'We take care of everything' wedding factory and did the whole wedding-in-a-box thing. It was the pull of thinking, *Wouldn't it be nice if I didn't have to worry about ridiculous things like whether I had remembered the forks? Wouldn't it be nice if I didn't have to hire a clean-up crew?*

And in the end, I think the wedding-in-a-box was not only easier for me, but also cheaper, and I think I still managed to make it very personalized and unique. In fact, I had more time to think about colors and flowers because I didn't have to think about basic logistics." —MARIE J.

"Our reception was at a country club, and I picked it because it was cost-effective and big enough for my giant family!" —JESSICA L.

"Our venue was exclusive for our party! Big bonus! Also the food menus were exactly what we were looking for. It definitely did not hurt that the prices were reasonable." —CHRISTINA M.

Ceremony Spaces

There aren't too many options when it comes to ceremony spaces; you can have a secular ceremony or a religious one. It can take place indoors or outdoors. You can have the ceremony at a site separate from the reception or at the same one.

If you belong to a religious institution or organization, you've always wanted to get married in your grandparents' church, or your father is a rabbi, you most likely already know who to contact. In a few calls, you'll be able to find out whether your date is available, who can perform the service, and how much all of it will cost.

Before you officially book your ceremony space, make sure you ask a few other questions, such as:

- Can you decorate the space?
- Is there a bridal room or suite?
- How many guests can fit comfortably in the space?
- Will the venue provide musicians and readers or will you have to?

- Can people who aren't practicing the religion attend?
- If the weather doesn't work out, will they move it indoors?

You don't need to invite everyone to your ceremony that you may invite to your reception—especially if it's a smaller space or will be a family-only affair. However, you should make sure to invite everyone to your reception that you invited to the ceremony. Otherwise, how will you ever get rid of them?

Tip!

If you choose to have your ceremony and reception at different locations, consider the distance between both sites. Will anyone need transportation? Is it possible anyone will get lost? If it's confusing, be sure to include directions with your invitations later!

Do you need an officiant?

Secular ceremony or not, you may need to bring or hire your own officiant. This sounds harder than it really is, I promise. Officiants are everywhere; you just need to know where to look.

They can be:

- Your family's or parish's priest or religious official
- A government official such as your town's judge, mayor, or justice of the peace
- An ordained friend or family member (think Howard and Bernadette's rooftop ceremony from *Big Bang Theory*, minus the Klingon—unless that's your thing!)

Anyone can do it. Visit The American Marriage Ministries (theamm.org), The Universal Life Church Monastery (themonastery.org), or various other websites to find out how.

Choosing the right person to officiate your ceremony is harder than actually finding someone qualified to do it. If you don't know them personally, you may want to interview them or ask them to get coffee or tea before booking them. This person sets the tone and pace of the entire ceremony—and sometimes everything else that follows. If you're planning on writing your own script or vows, including your friends or family, or you want to use specific readings, songs, etc., you need to know that the officiant is on board with all of it.

You also need to make sure they're comfortable speaking in front of a crowd. They need to be able to annunciate and project; they need to be heard. (Remember this as you recite your vows on your big day!)

Tip!

The officiant's duties don't always end after the ceremony. Make sure you and your officiant know what is required of each of you—paperwork, donations, travel, etc.

Reception Site

Traditionally, the ceremony and the reception take place on the same day. Sometimes, they take place in the same space. Once you get the business of the ceremony out of the way, then it's time to think about where you'll party!

With your tentative guest list and your style as a couple in mind, you can begin looking for venues. This can be

Is it ever too early to book a venue?

Katherine Cassell, event planner extraordinaire, says yes and no: "If you know that you absolutely love a venue and there is no chance of getting married anywhere else, then by all means you should book it—I emphasize this if you are getting married during one of the more popular months. However, especially when booking over a year in advance, I would highly recommend getting wedding/ event insurance. Most couples don't even know this exists but it is extremely helpful in situations where, say, your venue closes (due to bankruptcy, owner retiring, etc.), or your venue is damaged by a fire or an act of God. Wedding/ event insurance can start at prices less than $100 and can help couples recover money lost due to circumstances out of their hands."

tedious—finding information about various spaces, setting up appointments, and describing your vision for your big day over and over again is going to get frustrating—especially if you're picky.

And, trust me, you will quickly get sick of hearing about your cousin's friend of a friend who had her parents' anniversary party *there* and hated the entire experience. While other people can certainly weigh in, sometimes you have to physically visit the space and speak with the coordinators and event planners before you strike them from your list. (Maybe *they* thought your cousin's friend of a friend was the horrible one.)

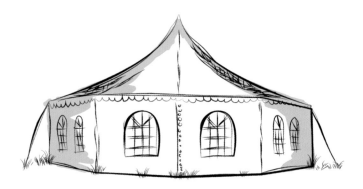

What Does the Reception Site Need to Provide?

When you meet with the planners and tour your potential venues, be sure you're upfront about everything you need from them. If you need the following, ask them if they provide it and how much it would cost:

- Cocktail hour space
- Food (dinner and cake)
- Alcohol/bar service
- Music
- Decorations
- Dance floor
- An on-site host/coordinator/planner

If you already have a caterer in mind, want to DIY decorate, and simply just want a space to celebrate, ask the site representative if they'll allow outside vendors. Find out what time your people could come and set up, how long you can keep the music going,

What is a wedding in a box?

If a friend says he or she used a wedding-in-a-box place, that simply means they found a venue or event space that offered the entire package for one, flat rate. Everything they needed, from music to photos to cake, was provided for them—they simply checked the boxes they wanted and the planner took care of the rest. If this sounds like something you're interested in, do some Googling and you'll come up with quite a few options, depending on where you live.

Event planner Katherine Cassell once worked at an all-inclusive venue such as this. Of booking this kind of wedding, she says, "I think they are a great idea if you are on a budget or if you like all of their options (typically an all-inclusive venue will have different packages that you can choose from depending upon what you would like and depending upon budget). I find that there is less room to personalize your wedding with all-inclusive vendors, however. For example, you may find a place whose menu you've fallen in love with, but when it comes to centerpieces, they may only allow you to choose a flower color scheme rather than actual flower types."

and if the venue will provide cleanup or if your people will have to come back the next morning to tidy up. Also be sure to ask about liability insurance, especially if you're planning on bringing in a bartender.

You'll find more information about booking vendors in chapter 5.

The Time Between

If you're having your ceremony and your reception on the same day, as most do, then you're also going to have to plan something else—the time spent between the ceremony and the reception.

As previously mentioned, if you're in two different locations, then you may have to arrange transportation for a few of the guests. Transportation to where, though? Will there be downtime between the ceremony and the reception? Will they go back to their hotels? Gather at your parents' house?

If you're in the same location, then your guests need somewhere to go and something to do once the ceremony ends. Can your venue accommodate cocktail hour directly after the ceremony? If the nuptials are short and the crowd is small, would they consider passing around champagne during the vows?

If you're going to have photos taken between the ceremony and the reception, then you have to be sure everyone outside of the wedding party is entertained—and that someone is in charge of said entertaining. Many couples today choose to do wedding photos before the ceremony or on an entirely different day, so they don't have this particular worry hanging over their heads. Something to think about!

5

Finding the Very Best Vendors

"Motto for the bride and groom: we are a work in progress
with a lifetime contract."
—PHYLLIS KOSS

• • •

*A*bout nine months to one year* before your wedding day,
you should start researching and meeting with potential
vendors who will help you bring together your big day.

These can be anyone from photographers to cake bakers,
lighting specialists to musicians, and everyone in between. Every
bride and groom has his and her own priorities, but most sources
agree you should book your vendors in the following order:

- Photographer
- Caterer
- Music (band/DJ)

---

*Or even earlier, if you can't wait to get started.

- Florist
- Cake maker/baker
- Videographer
- Transportation
- Decoration/design
- Rental agencies
- Invitation designers

Where will you find your vendors? If you're working with a wedding planner, he or she will have many connections in these fields and they'll happily point you in the right direction or even set up some meetings for you. If you don't have a planner (or even if you do), the planners or coordinators at your reception/ceremony sites may have recommendations (or even a list of vendors that you *have* to choose from, depending on your agreement with the site), as well as your friends, family members, and people you know in the businesses you'll be researching. You can also start searching for vendors online, specifically those located a reasonable distance from your ceremony or reception site.

Tip!

You should speak to representatives of at least two to three vendors per category. You need to know what's available to you, and you don't want to make a deal with the very first people you speak with. Just do yourself a favor and stop at three—if you don't go overboard, you'll avoid quite a bit of confusion and frustration (for you, the vendors, and your maid of honor).

Questions to Ask Your Vendors

Every interview with your potential vendors will be different, but there are some questions you're going to want to ask just about every one of them. These are:

- Are you available to work my date?
- How long have you been in business?
- What's been your most successful or memorable event?
- What should we expect the day of the wedding?
    - How many of your staff will attend?
    - If necessary, will there be someone on-site at all times?
    - If not on-site, will someone be on-call?
- How much is the deposit? What is the total balance?
- What is your cancellation policy?

Your online research will help you answer a lot of these questions before your interviews. Some people ask for lists of companies or satisfied customers the vendor has worked with in the past who they can call for a reference, but sometimes vendors are uncomfortable

---

Tip!

Be sure you connect with each vendor. If you get a weird/creepy vibe or you just *know* that you're not going to be able to depend on them when it comes to working efficiently and doing things on time, then don't sign on their dotted lines. This is, once again, one of the biggest days of your life—don't settle! If you don't trust a vendor, keep looking. One will turn up.

giving out that information. If you're looking for reviews, look no further than the Internet. If the business is fully developed (or even, sometimes, if it's not), you should be able to find people ranting and raving about just about everyone and everything.

When you've made your decision, be sure you have all the details down on paper and you keep all the dates and names of who you've spoken to and what their responses have been. As Mark O'Connell states in his book, *Modern Brides & Modern Grooms*, "Get everything in writing—even if it's just email—and be extremely explicit with anyone you ask for help. If you can't be explicit with a vendor or friend, find someone else."

Ask the Expert!
What is your best advice on working with outside vendors?

"Shop around, read reviews and listen to suggestions. If there is a band or DJ who plays at local venues (not for an event), go see them live to determine for yourself. If the catering company has a restaurant, go try them out for dinner. Fortunately for this generation, social media is a major factor especially when it comes to events. You can sift through different blogs or go on Instagram or Facebook to see a vendor's recent work. I think the most important thing to keep in mind is to make sure you trust your vendor and feel comfortable with what they have proposed. If you aren't feeling 100 percent compatible with them or their suggestions then see who else is out there." —KATHERINE CASSELL, NYC event planner

Before you sign any contracts with your vendors, be sure you read every word on every page. Don't expect your wedding planner, if you have one, to do it for you—unless he or she has specifically agreed to do so. If you have questions about your contract with your vendor, ASK!

Photographer

As we've previously discussed, many brides and grooms consider hiring a good photographer to be one of the most important—if not *the* most important—task on their wedding planning to-do list. After money spent on food and drinks, most of the average couple's budget goes toward photography. Photography services may take up 10 to 30 percent of your budget; expect to pay between $2,500 and $5,000 for some, and even higher for others.

Photography is such a big part of the day because it is the one thing that actually lasts—the one thing you can revisit time and again. You can share the photos with anyone, giving them a glimpse of your event if they weren't in attendance. Your dress will yellow, and you can only make so much room in the freezer for the top of your cake, but your memories of your wedding day will stick with you. As you grow older and those memories become a bit harder to recall, a quick glance at a wedding photograph on the hutch or in an album will surely bring you right back to that day.

The first step to finding a wedding photographer is to go through the prospective photographers' portfolios. Nearly all photographers have online portfolios showcasing samples of their work, so you should be able to get a good feel for what they may produce for you.

Tip!

Finding a photographer during the period of one year to nine months before your wedding is important because most photographers can only shoot one event per day—sometimes one per weekend if they have to travel or stay late into the night. Once someone else books your weekend, you're out of luck!

As you're sifting through one site after the other, bookmarking your favorites, consider what it is that you're looking for—what style of photographs do you want in your album? You should choose between traditional shots, which are mostly posed photos, or journalistic, which are more candid and capture the life of the party. (I'm a little biased here—journalistic all the way!) Or maybe, if you find the right photographer, you'll be able to do a little of both.

Once you have that answer, you should consider whether you want color photos, black-and-white photos, or both. Some photographers also offer options in sepia or color isolation.

When you narrow down your search and you're ready to meet with your top choices, be sure you're clear about what you're looking for and listen to them when they tell you what they can give you. If you're happy with what you're hearing, consider asking the following questions:

- Will multiple photographers be working the event?
  - If so, will they be shooting simultaneously?
  - Or will they take shifts?

- How many prints would you receive?
- How much will additional prints cost if you want more?
- How long will it take to develop?
- Will they be touching up the photos in any way?
- If so, will you get a preview before the finals are posted online or printed?
- Will you be allowed to share your photos online?

After you've finalized the booking and signed the contract, you won't be in touch with your photographer for a few months. About two months before the wedding, you should reach out and request a brief meeting to discuss the photographer(s) approach to shooting the event.

Before the meeting, sit down with your partner and make a list of the must-have photos you want of your day. Maybe you don't care so much about cutting the cake, and maybe you're not doing the traditional garter and bouquet toss, but you *really* want a photo of the father-daughter dance or each person brave enough to give a toast. Or maybe you really want to avoid the table-by-table group shots and would rather he or she focus on your friends and family killing it on the dance floor.

Videographers

Traditionally, booking a videographer is less of a priority than a photographer, but sometimes you can find them at the same time! Your photographer may not employ a videographer, nor be one him or herself, but they most likely can point you in the right direction of one they know and respect.

When you're interviewing your potential video-graphers, be sure to ask them:

- How many people are on your crew?
- If multiple, how many will be attending your ceremony? Your reception?
- How many hours of video will they be shooting?
- What is the price per hour?
- In what format will they deliver the finished video? (CD, removable hard drive, online file transfer, etc.)
- Will they be asking friends and family to speak on camera, or will they avoid interviews?
- Do they have experience working an event simultaneously with a photographer?

This last question is important, as you want to make sure that the photographer and videographer are not going to get in each other's way. If you're booking both of these professionals, ask if they'd be open to meeting with you together or having a conference call to discuss their approaches, your wish list, and how to go about making it perfect.

Caterer

Once you have a photographer booked, you can relax a bit—and then book your caterer.

As discussed in chapter 4, your caterer may come with your venue. It's inarguably more difficult to work with a caterer outside of your venue; however, the pros of this situation can definitely outweigh the cons. The right caterer will allow you to plan the perfect menu— one that speaks of you as a couple or of your culture, one that can accommodate dietary restrictions without sacrificing quality. Your relationship with your caterer is important, as

each of your guests will be eating the food provided, meaning the meal can have a lasting impact on all attendees.

Before you begin your search for caterers, you should decide what type of menu you're looking for. The time of day, as well as the length of your reception, may affect this. Which meal will you be providing your guests? Brunch or lunch? Dinner? Just dessert? Curiously, brunch weddings and dessert weddings are gaining popularity at the time of this writing.

Once you figure out the type of menu you'd like to offer guests, then you have to choose the way the food will be served. Will guests be able to make their own plates at a buffet or will they pass each item around the table, family-style? Or would you rather it be more formal wherein guests are seated and they receive one plate per course each?

And speaking of courses, how many would you like to serve? Your options include: appetizers, salads, soups, pasta, fruits and cheeses, entrée, and desserts.

Additional questions you should be asking yourself before contacting a caterer include:

- What type of entrée should we offer? Meats, pasta, seafood, vegetarian, or vegan?
- What is our palate? Ethnic, comfortable, regional, seasonal?
- Will there be food during cocktail hour?
- What do we want the food we choose to say about us?
- Will there be alcohol?

As we discussed earlier, your wedding is your day, and if you don't drink and would rather your guests not consume alcohol on your day, then by all means—have a dry wedding. If that's going to make you happy, then they can deal for the day.

However, if you're going to offer your guests alcohol at your reception. The following box contains a few tips.

Drink Up!

Some questions to ask yourself when you consider having a bar at your wedding include:

Who will bartend?

- If you're going to offer alcohol at your wedding and the bartender is not provided by the venue, ask your caterer if he or she has a bartender on staff. For bigger groups, ask if they have more than one bartender who could work the event.

- If a friend of a friend knows a bartender, be sure he or she is licensed or has some type of certification and liability insurance.

How much will we need?

- If it's open bar, The Knot suggests the following, per 100 people: 18 bottles of champagne, 10 bottles of red wine, 18 bottles of white wine, 2 to 3 cases of beer (and various other liters of whiskey, gin, rum, vodka, cranberry and orange juice, and club soda)
- If you're only serving during the toast and dinner, then, per 100 people, The Knot suggests: 18 bottles of champagne and 50 bottles of wine.

Who will supply the necessary tools and glasses?

- The bartender should have his or her own mixers, shakers, tongs, etc. Check with the catering company to see if they will supply the glassware. Ask about any extra fees for this.

How can we save money in this area?

- If a bottle is open, even for just one drink or shot, you have to pay for it—and so ends the rules of open bar. However, if you create multiple signature cocktails for your reception and limit guests to said cocktails, white and red wine, and perhaps beer, then you'll save some cash.

Is a cash bar acceptable?

- Short answer? No. Long answer: Yes, but you may have to deal with some complaints and "jokes."

After deciding on your palate and your general plans for your event's food and drinks, you should also figure out what you need from your caterer that your venue is not providing. This includes bar service and alcohol, the cake, service/waitstaff, on-site management, and rentals ranging from dinnerware to tables and even Sternos.

Once you've made all your notes, contact your top three potential caterers to set up meetings and sample tastings. Discuss your ideas with them, request sample menus, and don't forget to ask:

- Does the catering service have liability insurance? Are you expected to get it?
- Have they ever worked with your venue before?
- How many people will work the event? What is the breakdown between staff making the food and staff serving the food?
- Will someone be on-site the entire time?
- How will they coordinate setup, serving courses, and cleanup?
- What happens with the leftover food?
- Any additional questions about bar service, cutting the cake, and rentals.

When you've chosen your caterer and signed an agreement, agree to stay in touch with ideas about the menu as you get them. Make an appointment for six to eight weeks before your wedding to taste the food they plan on serving.

Planning Your Menu

You don't need to have a set menu in mind the day you sign the contract with your caterer. You should definitely have an idea of which meal you'll be serving and which setup you'd like to use (banquet, family style, full service, etc.), but you don't need to know exactly what should be on each plate. This comes after much consideration of the following factors:

- You don't want the main meal to be too heavy, as you won't want your guests to feel too full or weighed down. This will make them sleepy and may keep them off the dance floor.
- The food shouldn't be messy unless it fits your theme. If you're all for Southern barbeque and you've got a smoker full of pork in the backyard, then make sure you have a lot of napkins handy. However, if the event is a black-tie affair, steer clear of any foods that may drip or require guests to use their hands.
- Many generations may be present at your wedding, so your food needs to be appropriate for every age group. It shouldn't be too difficult or confusing to eat and ingredients shouldn't be too crazy. People are picky about what they will and will not eat (many are more than hesitant to try anything new), so keep it simple for all palates so everyone can enjoy.
- Don't forget the kids. You may need to create a kids menu if you have many in attendance.

Remember, the caterer is the professional in this situation. They know the cost of particular ingredients, they understand seasonal flavors and spices. You should trust their judgment; if they tell you a specific flavor combination won't work, it most likely won't work. Again, the food at your reception is important, as *everyone* in attendance will be eating it. Every guest won't dance, nor will every guest have cake, but every one of them will come expecting to be fed. Don't disappoint them!

At the time of your tasting, all the ingredients the caterer plans on using at your reception should be in season so everything they serve you as a sample should match what they will serve your guests. Pay attention to the presentation of the food on the plate, the portion sizes, the taste of each element on your plate (separately and together), and the timing between courses.

Working with an outside caterer doesn't have to be difficult!

Advice from Jolene Guignet, married 2015

How'd you find your caterer?

Our venue had a list of approved caterers. There were about twelve on the list. We were free to use whoever we wanted, but then we would have to pay a nonrefundable $500 deposit. We decided it was best to go with one of their caterers because they would be familiar with the venue. After that, I began emailing different people with a general idea of what I was looking for, the amount of people, and the date. I was sent multiple proposals, which I cataloged into a spreadsheet so that I could easily evaluate them.

Did you taste test before you signed a contract?

No. We did a few taste tests at other places, but only met with the woman from our caterer. [This caterer doesn't] do taste tests until closer to the wedding because of menu changes. We did read their reviews and really, really liked the woman who is working with us, so we went with them before tasting.

Did you have to obtain any type of license/liability insurance or did the caterer have one?
The caterer has insurance.

Are you also bringing in an outside bartender?
The caterer provides the bartender as part of our catering package. Our venue only provides the building, tables, and chairs, so our caterer is "full service." They do a lot of things and act as our day-of coordinator.

Cake Baker

If your caterer or venue does not include a cake in their packages, they may be able to point you toward bakers they've worked with in the past who have produced impressive and delicious wedding cakes. Your florist may also have baking connections, as bakers and florists often work together at various events.

If a baker is popular and in-demand in your area, you may want to sign a contract with them up to six months before your wedding. If they're just starting out or have a large staff and can manage multiple events, you may be able to book them up to three months out.

Like photographers, you can see bakers' best works online, which means you can also find reviews of their cakes. Click around, talk to your friends, and decide what type of cake (or cakes) that you want before contacting your top three. Talk to your potential bakers about flowers and fillings, icing, decorations, and any custom elements you have always envisioned on your wedding cake.

Questions to ask your baker before signing a contract include:

- What is your history with working on wedding cakes?
- How fresh will my cake be?
  - If it's finished early, how will it be stored?
- Will there be a delivery charge?
  - How will the cake be delivered?
  - When will it arrive at the reception site?
- How much will be edible?

Feel free to get references, ask for a taste of the flavors you think you want, and query about alternative cakes—cupcakes, cake pops, his-and-her cakes, vegan/gluten-free cakes, etc.

When you're deciding how big of a cake you will need, remember that you do *not* need a slice of cake per guest. Many guests will not eat your cake, either because they will have left

right after the cake cutting (a popular time to say goodnight) or they lack a sweet tooth (… weird, I know).

Something to keep in mind: if you're working with an outside baker, check with your venue to see if they will charge you to cut and serve the cake. This happens more often than you think, so be sure you know of this fee up front so you can plan for it.

Ask the Expert

Lei Shishak started her culinary career in New York City, graduating top of her class from the Culinary Institute of America. After culinary school, she moved to California, where she worked next to award-winning chefs and made a name for herself in the pastry arts. Today, Lei is a cookbook author and owner of Sugar Blossom Bake Shop in San Clemente, California. In addition to cupcakes and cookies appropriate for any type of beach gathering, Lei and her staff also make wedding cakes. She has taken a few seconds out of her busy schedule to explain her bakery's process when working with brides and grooms to make their dream wedding cakes.[1]

What would you advise couples to know/decide before they contact a baker?

It's really helpful when couples do some research and have a discussion beforehand. Determining their preferences for basic things such as colors, frosting (butter cream versus fondant), and flowers (type of, real versus fake) before contacting me makes the process more efficient. If a couple isn't exactly sure what they want the cake to look like, it helps to know what feeling they want their cake to evoke (e.g., romantic and sexy,

---

1 To learn more about Lei Shishak and Sugar Blossom Bake Shop, visit www.SugarBlossomBakeShop.com.

delicate and virginal, show-stopping WOW, classy and formal, vintage retro, etc).

How does the typical wedding cake consultation progress?

The process typically starts with a phone call or email exchange during which I retrieve basic information such as desired cake flavors, colors, design, tiers, and servings. We then schedule a tasting appointment that's held at my bakery. After they sample cake flavors of their choosing, I sit down with them and take detailed notes of what they like and what they don't like. We'll also peruse photos of cakes to determine a final cake design. Within twenty-four hours, I email the couple a detailed quote and sketch of the cake and hopefully win their business!

What do you find to be the most challenging part about this process?

The most challenging part is understanding a couple's expectations. I ask a lot of detailed questions during the tasting because I want to make sure I not only meet but also exceed their wedding cake expectations.

What is your favorite part about creating wedding cakes?

When I am making a couple's wedding cake, I love to imagine their surprise and joy when they see it on their wedding day.

Friends & Family

If your friends and family members like to cook and they're more than willing to do so for your special occasion, don't be afraid to ask for their help so you don't need to book caterers, bakers, or bartenders. In this case, you'll probably need to work more with rental agencies and you'll want to increase your wedding insurance (unless everyone contributing happens to be a professional), but at least you'll know you can absolutely trust the people providing the food and drinks.

Because it's your day and you're calling the shots, don't be afraid to be critical—but do it in the nicest way possible. If Aunt Shelly is bringing her mac-n-cheese and you know that the last time you had it, it had too much pepper in it, suggest she consider cutting back a bit. If your mother thinks her best cake is red velvet, but you really want lemon, be firm. If your brother volunteers to grill, but your dad is really the family's grill master, ask your brother to hand over the tongs or ask your dad to supervise. If your bridesmaid wants to bake cookies, and no one's ever said anything nice about her cookies, let her down easy and give her another task.

A family affair could be a great thing as long as everyone's on the same page. Call a meeting for everyone contributing and make sure they know exactly what they've signed up for. Talk about transporting the food, setup, and how it will be served. Talk about cleanup. And thank them, profusely, for their help. (And, if it's in your budget, maybe take them out for dinner or drinks or make sure they get a special favor.)

Entertainment

Many couples put the importance of good and fun entertainment up there with delicious food and great photographs. Hearing certain songs undoubtedly brings up memories, and that's why choosing the right songs and having them played at the perfect moments is something many couples stress over. After choosing a playlist that speaks of your relationship and will be fun for everyone in attendance, you shouldn't need to be worry about executing that playlist—and that's why you need to find the right entertainer(s) to get the party started and keep it going.

You have four options when it comes to music: a DJ, a band, a DJ and a band, or someone with an iPod. That last one is admittedly probably best for an after-party; however, if you're trying to keep it simple—and there's absolutely nothing wrong with doing so—it could be a good choice.

Before you start your research here, decide what you want out of your musical choice. Do you think your crowd would appreciate the live music, or do you think they'd be better off with lots of bass, some hip-hop, and a few crazy lights?

Once you figure that out, you can start searching for local bands and DJs. If you find something you like online, or if a friend suggests you may be interested in a particular act, you

should go see them in person. Never sign a contract with a musical act you only see online; you need to see them in their element and you need to see how they work a crowd. If their onstage antics are inappropriate or they can only perform when they're drunk or high, move on. You don't need that drama at your wedding reception, no matter how good their music may be.

Bands are always going to be more expensive than DJs because you're hiring a group of people rather than one man or woman and his/her equipment. The lead singer of the group will most likely act as your emcee, so when you go to see them play, pay attention to his or her personality and the way he or she interacts with the room during their set and after they've finished playing.

This also applies to DJs; when you go to an event they're working, be sure they can work the room and get people on the dance floor. You don't want their personality to be overbearing, though—no one should be embarrassed or feel forced to be on the floor. If they're not comfortable dancing, they don't need to dance and shouldn't feel pressured to do so. That's not fun for anyone.

Aside from being cheaper than a band, another benefit of a DJ over a band would be the variety of music the DJ may be able to play. Some bands don't know or won't cover some of the songs you want, nor will they change their sound to fit the mood of your event. When a band takes a break during your reception, they may not have any music to play in the interim; a DJ can set a playlist and walk away if he or she needs to.

Once you've decided whether you want a band or a DJ (or both) and you've gone to see them play, it's time to talk to your top choices. Be sure to ask the following of both:

- When will they arrive and how long will they need to set up?
- Will they need help setting up or do they have their own crew?
- When will they start playing? How long will they play?

- Will take they take breaks? And if so, how many and for how long?
- What does their library look like?
- Will they learn/purchase new songs for your reception?
- Will they take requests from your guests?
- If you've decided to (or your venue has offered to) provide an emcee for the night, can they work with that person throughout the night?

Two to three months before your wedding, send a playlist to your band or DJ. The playlist should contain must-play songs as well as do-not-play (Chicken Dance, anyone?) songs. Make sure you're clear about which songs you'd like played and when. Events that you may want to consider specific songs for include:

- Entrance
- First dance
- Father/daughter dance
- Mother/son dance
- Grandmother/father dances
- Traditional/custom/ religious/cultural dances
- Last dance

Try not to change your mind too often on these songs, as it might get confusing for everyone involved.

Tip!

If you decide to hire both a band and a DJ, decide when each will play. Maybe the band will only play during cocktail hour, or they're alternate based on what's going on during the reception. Be sure to put them in touch with one another so they can coordinate.

Other Forms of Entertainment

If you have the budget to work with, you can offer more than just music as entertainment at your reception. Of course, some of these options may be a better fit at the bridal shower or rehearsal dinner, but every wedding is different and you should make it your own in any way you can.

Additional forms of entertainment may include:

- **Photo slideshow**—maybe the two of you have been together for a while or have traveled the world and have some amusing photos to share with your guests.
- **Interactive displays**—asking your guests to participate in your day in some way can put a nice spin on it. Have them write you a letter to open in the future, sign a guest book, vote on favorite photos, enter a caption contest, etc. Be creative with it.
- **Games**—set up a survey to see who knows you best, play mix and match games with photos, turn your wedding into a scavenger hunt with a special prize for the winner.
- **Photo booth**—this is extremely popular these days. You can rent a photo booth and props from various vendors, have the photos uploaded online, and guests can view and download them later.
- **Acts**—maybe your partner is a fan of a specific college team and you've asked the mascot to come

say hi; maybe you've hired professional ballet dancers to perform during the band's break; maybe your wedding is circus-themed and you've managed to book an animal trainer. The possibilities are only endless if you consider your budget!

- **Performances**—maybe the groom wrote a song for the occasion and he wants to debut it; maybe your blended family wants to perform a dance number; maybe you want to let your hair down and sing a bit.
- **Venue-provided entertainment**—if your venue has the goods, be sure they're on display! A friend of mine attended a wedding last year at a zoo on the west coast. Guests were able to walk the grounds, meet giraffes, and take pictures with monkeys.
- **Fireworks**—if you have the space and it won't disturb neighbors, a fireworks display could make for a perfect and romantic end of the night. Just be sure you hire professionals to set them off.

Florist

Flowers may not seem important to everyone at first (me, included), but once you start to talk to vendors, your wedding party, and your mother, you'll soon see that they are—and that even if you don't know the name of the flowers you want, someone else does.

Many couples use flowers to set the tone of the wedding and to tie the color scheme together. A big, beautiful bouquet and fresh boutonnieres bring a certain sophistication that would be lacking if men were missing these pieces on their tuxes and the bridesmaids' bouquets were wilted.

To find a florist, you can search online or speak with your baker, who most likely has a few on speed dial from past projects, or you can ask your venue if they have any recommendations. While speaking with the event planner at the venue, be sure to confirm that it's okay to bring outside décor.

Once you've narrowed down your choices, make a list of all the people who will need flowers (bridesmaids, groomsmen, mothers, flower girl) and in what forms (respectively: bouquets, boutonnieres, corsages, petals), and all the places you'll put them during the ceremony and reception (on the altar, in an arch at the end of the aisle, on the pews or chairs, as a runner down the aisle, table arrangements and centerpieces, etc.).

I won't go into detail about types of flowers, what they mean, which season is best, etc., as there are tons of books and Internet sites to help you make these decisions. I can, however, help you with bouquet shapes. While corsages and boutonnieres are pretty straightforward, you're going to have to think a little bit about the shape of your bouquet, as well as your bridesmaids'. The most popular shapes include:

- **Cascade**—also known as a waterfall bouquet, these bouquets spill down and hang.
- **Hand-tied**—a favorite of DIY brides; these are a simple and loose gathering of flowers tied with a ribbon.
- **Nosegay**—a small, round cluster of flowers tied with a bow. Another DIY favorite.
- **Pomander**—also known as a Victorian Kissing Ball; tightly packed pall of flowers suspended from a looped ribbon to be worn on the wrist.
- **Round**—traditionally round, larger, and can be made with any of flower.

Tip!

Stay away from wearing flowers that may need to be in water to thrive; these will quickly wilt. Also, ask your florist which types of flowers may wilt if they are handled or touched. These are clearly not flowers you'll want to work with on your wedding day.

Now that you know how many flowers you need, what types and shapes, what's in season, and what makes you sneeze, you can make appointments with your top florists. You should try to book a florist no later than nine months before your wedding. However, it's a good idea to make an appointment around a year before the wedding to see what's in season the month of your wedding.

During your appointments with your potential florists, ask as many questions as you need to, including:

- How many other events are you working that day or weekend?

- Do you anticipate any issues with X number of events?
- How will delivery be handled?
  - When will the flowers arrive?
- Will you need assistance setting up?
- What do you suggest we do with the leftover flowers?

After meeting, they will make you a sample arrangement based on what you've told them you're envisioning. This is the time to be honest, so give truthful—but polite—feedback.

Tip!

If you plan on throwing your bouquet into the arms of an awaiting mob of women, but you're also attached to the idea of keeping and preserving your wedding-day bouquet, get a second, smaller one made. This way, you can toss the small one and keep the one that made the trip down the aisle with you.

Decorations

If you're working with a wedding planner, event planner, or event designer, this is most likely where they're going to take the lead. You'll see diagrams and sketches and spreadsheets while they coordinate with the florist, lighting professionals, and rental agencies.

Your designer or decorator will also work closely with the reception manager or representative, as they've seen their space used in various ways and have valuable feedback about what has worked in the past and what hasn't. The decorator will also want to work with the reception manager to make sure everything they have planned (lighting, hanging any structures from the ceiling, lighting candles, etc.) is approved and doesn't violate any fire codes or lines in your contract.

This is the time to think about your dance floor (how much room do you need? what materials will you use?), the setup of your tables (sweetheart table? wedding party up front? square or circle?), and the various stations you'd like to feature. You should also map out a tentative seating chart based on your tentative guest list, as well as your floral arrangements.

Though you're most likely handing over the reins a bit in this area, you can still find a way to save money. Ask your decorator (whether she's your younger sister with big ideas or a professional florist who has worked hundreds of events) to entertain your budget-friendly ideas and be open to their responses, as sometimes you really do get what you pay for.

A few easy ways to save some money on décor include:

- Keeping the design and decorations simple, clean, and elegant
- Transporting the decorations used at the ceremony site to the reception site
- Picking ceremony and reception sites that are stunning or unique, requiring less decoration
- Skip personalizing every single piece of décor
- DIY as much as you can, from centerpieces to chair covers to setup the day before the event

What was your most memorable decoration at your ceremony/reception?

"I framed famous quotes for each table. And made candle lanterns for center pieces. We had a memorial candle, too." —ARDI A.

"We had a candle lit with a printed piece of paper saying 'If heaven weren't so far away, we know you'd be here' on an empty seat during our ceremony to represent our loved ones that had passed away." —STACY K.

"We had this amazing fruit tree, I guess you would call it. The trunk was made of pineapples (tops cut off) stacked on top of each other and fruit was skewered (toothpicked, I guess) onto the trunk in, like, a swirly pattern." —MELISSA L.

"Definitely our memorial table. We had a rose for each of our grandparents that had passed in a vase, and mini picture frames with their pics around it with a poem. I was really close to my nana, so it really meant a lot to me." —LYNN M.

Transportation

Sometimes transportation is overlooked until the last minute. The invitations are out, guests are RSVPing, and suddenly everyone needs to know where they're going, how they're getting there, and, once they arrive, where they're parking. Don't wait too long to figure this all out. Book your drivers and cars six to eight months before the wedding.

Who needs a ride and where are they going?

To the ceremony:
Most likely, you're going to want to offer transportation for you and your partner, your wedding party, and possibly your immediate family. You may also want to have vehicles available for older guests who cannot transport themselves.

From the ceremony to the reception:
This will not be an issue if your ceremony and reception are happening at the same site. However, if there's some distance between these two locations, then you'll need to consider transportation for you and your partner, your wedding party, your family, and older guests.

Say your sites are within a walkable distance, the weather is agreeable, and terrain is easy, some of your guests may choose to saunter down to the reception site if they're wearing comfortable shoes. Find out before you book your transportation if anyone either 1) won't be using the vehicles provided or 2) cannot cross the distance between sites and needs transportation.

From the reception:
If your reception is in or on the grounds of a hotel, you may not need the same amount of vehicles for this trip. Also, many guests may choose to carpool depending on where family and friends are heading after the party. If your bridesmaid Carol came with you in the limousine from the ceremony site, but is staying with a bunch of mutual friends from high school, then she'll most likely leave in their car instead of taking the limo with the rest of the party.

What will you use?

Ask around and do research to find the name of a respectable and affordable company. They may use limousines, town cars, or other types of luxury vehicles. Depending on the company, they may also rent horses and carriages, model cars, or cars from particular eras that may match your theme.

Questions to ask the transportation company include:

- Is the tip included in the final bill?
- Can you coordinate drop-off and pick-up times?
  - If not, will they be onsite the entire time of the party for those who want to leave early?
- Will the driver have GPS accessible to him/her?
  - Will they be provided with directions?
  - Should you be expected to know the directions in case the driver gets lost?
- What type of add-ons are included in the cost?
  - If none, what does it cost to add items such as chilled champagne and soda?

If a transportation company is not within your budget, or you simply won't need a number of cars, you could always ask your friends and family for help. Determine how many guests need transportation and then determine how many guests have open seats in their cars and are able to offer a ride or two. This may take a few phone calls, emails, and back and forth. This is a task you can most likely hand off to your bridesmaids or groomsmen to complete.

Tip!

You may be able to get a discount with a transportation company if you use them more than once. If you agree to book them for your bridal shower and/or bachelorette/bachelor party, then they may give you a returning/loyal customer discount or may allow you to bundle all services together for a cut in cost.

Parking

When booking your ceremony and reception sites, remember that guests will need convenient parking. Ask to see the parking lots and definitely consider the implications if the ceremony site, specifically, doesn't have either a lot for parking or a private lot. If attendees are going to need to circle the block to look for on-street parking, let them know so they aren't late for the ceremony. If the lot is small, consider inviting fewer people to the ceremony.

If the reception site's lot is large—so large that it may have multiple levels, as per some lodges or country clubs—ask if you could reserve a specific number of close spots, either for VIP and handicapped guests or for the entire party. This way, no one needs to walk a mile, possibly in the dark, to get to their cars after hours of dancing.

For weddings taking place during the rainy season or in the winter months, ask the ceremony or reception site managers how they take care of their lots. Will they keep them clean of snow and ice? If there's a chance of rain or snow on your wedding day, ask the reception managers if there is a specific drop-off zone where guests and vendors can unload under an awning or protection of some type.

Other Vendors

The next few vendors you will most likely work with are on a smaller scale, though that doesn't mean they're any less important. They're going to be easy to work with, and your options will be varied. It all comes down to who you already know and your taste/style/ideas for your big day.

Rental agencies

Once you've booked your venue, your caterer, your bartender, your baker, and worked with your decorator or reception manager on the setup you'll be using, you'll have a good idea of what you may need to rent. When you're working with each of these vendors, be sure to ask about the equipment they're bringing and make a note of what they are not providing so you can rent it.

Before you choose any rental agency (you may end up using more than one), be sure to do your research and find out if the company is dependable and how their prices compare to others in the area. If you're looking to rent something specific, you may be limited in your options, but if you keep your list general, you may find many who will suit your needs. You'll want to finish up your contract with rental agencies four to five months before your wedding.

Items you may need to rent include, but are not limited to:

- Chairs/chair covers
- Tables
  - For dinner
  - For food stations
  - For features
- Linens
- Dinnerware
  - Forks, spoons, knives
  - Glasses, coffee cups
  - Plates, bowls, butter dishes, gravy boats
- Barware
  - Various bar glasses, including champagne flutes and tumblers
  - Swizzle sticks, cocktail napkins
- Tools for food service, bar service, and cake cutting
- Stage for the band/DJ

Once you've signed your contracts with all your vendors, back off for a little while and breathe. If you've hired a wedding planner, they may maintain contact with each vendor and get you involved as little as possible if that's what you wish. If you're without a planner, consider dividing your vendors between your wedding party and ask each person to manage that vendor. Call only when you have real questions, try to stick to the schedule you have set, and don't bother them unless it's an emergency. Remember, you've hired professionals. Treat them with respect and they will return the favor.

6

Dress Shopping

"There is no greater feeling than when a groom turns to see his
bride and has tears in his eyes because she is so beautiful."
—TIM ALAN

• • •

M any women refer to their wedding gowns as the only
things that really matter about their weddings. Of course,
this isn't true of every bride, but even if you haven't been
thinking about your own wedding dress since you first married
your Barbie off to Ken, you're probably excited about the dress
shopping process now!

Before we get into different types of skirts, veils, and various
accessories, there's one important thing to remember now more
than ever:

It's your day. Wear what you want.

If you don't want to wear a wedding dress, please—don't
wear a wedding dress! Buy a cocktail dress or a skirt or whatever

you want. Don't even wear a dress if you don't want to. If a suit or tux is more your thing, go for it. If you don't want to wear white, don't wear white. If you're really proud of your body and you want to show off all your hard work, then show it off! Don't worry about defending your choice of attire; just wear what is going to make you feel comfortable and good about yourself. Wear what you feel represents *you*.

What if your mother, father, or grandmother is paying for and wants you to wear lace or cover up your chest? Out of respect for them, consider their feelings, entertain their opinions, but at the end of the day, if they have told you to choose the dress you really want, then purchase the dress that fits you best—physically and emotionally.

First Steps

Before we go any further, you need to do two things: 1) set a budget and, whatever you do, do NOT look at any dresses that are more expensive than the price you've set and 2) determine whether you have enough time to order a dress and get alterations made or whether you'll have to buy off the rack. If you want to get your dress altered so that it looks the best it can on you, then consider dress shopping nine months to one year before your wedding.

Once you know how much you can spend and when to go shopping, you can start thinking about what type of dress to buy.

> ## Tip!
>
> You may also want to wait until you have a venue booked before you purchase your wedding attire. Your venue, along with the date you choose, may affect the type of dress you choose. If you're having a winter wedding, you may need a heavier material or certain accessories to stay warm. If you've decided to get married on the beach, you may want a shorter skirt to stay out of the sand and a lightweight fabric.

If you feel like the Internet, books, magazines, etc., will be confusing and want to talk to someone in the business about dresses and their accessories, you could reach out to a professional and ask for a meeting or some advice.

Sara Brosious of Sara Brosious Custom Bridal is one of those professionals, and her advice will guide us through this section. After spending some time in the womenswear industry and working for brands such as Rebecca Taylor and Walter Baker, she created her own luxury womenswear brand. A few years later, her interests had shifted and she found herself in the wedding world—gowns, bridesmaids' dresses, and ties for groomsmen were among the first of her products. She enjoys working with brides who know *exactly* what they're looking for, as well as those who aren't sure and haven't even browsed the racks yet.[2]

---

2 You can find out more about Sara's business at http://sarabrosious.com/. Feel free to email Sara at sara@sarabrosious.com.

Your Dress: Style, Bits, and Pieces

If you've been pinning wedding dresses for a while, you may be able to skip this section. However, if you don't quite know what you're getting yourself into, or you just need a little refresher, let me break it down for you as simply as I can. Knowing the names of these pieces will help you tell your future dress consultant what you're looking for—and what you definitely don't want.

First thing's first: determine your style. This will most likely match the style you've decided for your wedding, be it romantic or traditional/classical. You may also be thinking of vintage, princess, or something more glamorous.

Tip!

Some women want to discuss anything but their dress or dress shopping experiences because they're not comfortable with their bodies. They want to wait until they lose weight to start shopping, they start crazy diets, and they worry about the number on the tag—the size, not the price.

An important thing to realize when you start dress shopping is that body type and weight are totally different here. Your weight may fluctuate; you may gain weight or lose weight at any time. However, your body type will *never* change. If you're pear-shaped, you're pear-shaped. If you're short, you're short. There's nothing you can do about your body type, so you may as well accept it and shop for it.

Buy the dress that's right for your body, not your current or ideal weight.

Silhouettes

Once you have a hold of your personal style, consider the gown silhouette that fits your body best and you're most comfortable with. The most popular gown silhouettes include:

Mini *If you'll be traipsing through the sand or want to show some leg, this one's for you!*	
A-line *Common, somewhat safe, but sure to make you look good, no matter your body type.*	
Mermaid *Sexy, fitted from the bust to the knees, and perfect for athletic brides.*	

Princess (or ball gown) *Better for full-figured or pear-shaped brides; essentially an A-line cut with a bit more poof.*	
Empire *A loose fit, comfortable with lots of flow; not quite right for those with larger busts.*	
Column *Known to be clingy or constricting if you don't have the tall, lean body for it; might make dancing, eating, and possibly even breathing difficult if doesn't fit just right.*	
Fit-and-flare *As it sounds, fitted from the bust to the hips and then flares out from there.*	

True Religion

If your ceremony, or event in general, is going to showcase your religion, you should keep this in mind while dress shopping. If you religion requires you to dress modestly, the column, fit-and-flare, mermaid, or mini silhouettes are most likely out of the question. Necklines may also come into play here.

Think about your traditions and customs when shopping for accessories, as well. You may need to purchase additional items such as gloves or a shawl.

Length

We've already touched on length a bit, so you know this may be determined by your location. Otherwise, this decision is most likely going to be based on personal preference—and whether you have some rockin' calves or ankles!

Your gown length may be:

- **Ballerina**—just above the ankles
- **Floor**—right to the floor
- **Hi-lo**—shorter in the front, to the floor in the back
- **Short**—at the knee or even above (think: cocktail dress)
- **Tea**—just below the knees

Neckline

Choosing your neckline may also mean keeping your family's traditions and your grandmother's requests in mind. But, as we've discussed, if you want a specific cut—one you've always envisioned—put your foot down and don't pick it up!

- **Halter**—This may support you if you have a large bust, but may also put pressure on the back of your neck and shoulders, so it may not be the most comfortable option. Also, it brings a lot of attention to the shoulders and arms.
- **Scoop**—This works for nearly every bride, as you can choose how high or low you'd like the neckline to scoop.
- **Square**—Another safe option that works for every bust; the cut features ninety-degree angles and thick straps.
- **Strapless**—Classic, an easy fit for most brides, but especially popular with athletic brides with toned arms and shoulders.
- **Sweetheart**—Strapless, heart-shaped, supportive, and great for women with larger busts.
- **V-Neck**—Similar to the scoop neckline, V-necks are popular with many brides, as you can choose how far you'd like it to plunge.

Skirt

These may be details you've already decided you're in love with or that you absolutely hate, you just never knew exactly how to express those feelings. Let's consider these new vocabulary words:

- **Tiers**—layers of fabric of varying lengths
- **Streamers**—fabric, cut into thick or thin strings, that may hang from the gown, most likely down the back
- **Petals**—a new section of skirt, typically placed on top of the main skirt and in a different fabric

- **Draping**—pulling the fabric of the skirt to the side or to the back, creating a more full effect; this detail may also feature pleats
- **Pleats**—fabric folded in specific areas of the skirt
- **Bustles**—gathering of fabric at the back of the gown, typically fastened with hooks or buttons
- **Flounce**—placement of a large, obvious ruffle at the base of the skirt
- **Tails**—layers, or panels, of the same fabric that follow behind the gown, similar to a train

Trains and Veils

While you can't get around thinking about your silhouette, the length of your dress, your skirt, and your neckline, you don't have to wear a train or a veil if you don't want to. You can go without the train, and there are plenty of alternatives to veils (headbands, bows, flowers, hair combs, tiaras, or barrettes).

Keep in mind that when you speak of veils, many may assume that you're speaking of trains—but there's a difference. According to Sara Brosious, that difference is simple:

A bridal train is the part of a wedding gown that "trains" behind the bride. The term bridal gown *originates from the word* al, *which means "party," combined with* bride, *i.e. "Bride's Party Gown." The train varies in length depending on the style of the dress. Trains add a touch of majesty to a wedding. Brides look (and feel) almost regal as they flow past with the ornamental train trailing behind them. The train also helps to further differentiate your gown from the bridesmaids' dresses.*

Trains make a dramatic accent to your dress, especially when you can take portraits with it swirled around you on the floor.

A veil is a fashion accessory intended to cover some part of the head or face and to compliment the dress. The length of the veil often relates to the formality of the ceremony. As a custom bridal designer, I believe that brides don't have to follow strict rules any longer and should have the freedom to wear whatever type of veil they desire. Personally, I feel that a bride should evaluate the key focal point of her dress before picking out a veil. The veil should not cover the focal point or take away attention from it. If the bride prefers a longer veil, I would recommend a sheer style that does not cover up the details of the dress.

Trains

Trains are a great way to bring your own personal style to your wedding dress. If you want to feel like a princess, something long and flowing may fit your big day. If you want to have a great time on the dance floor without worrying about tripping over your dress, something shorter will be perfect.

- **Brush**—Also called a sweep, this is one of the shorter trains and may be as long as 18 inches from the gown. This style works best on slim-fitting gowns.
- **Court**—Similar to a brush train, this one also stretches 18 inches from the gown, but fastens at the hip or the waist.
- **Watteau**—Similar to a cape, and sometimes called a capelet, this train is fastened at the shoulders and stretches to the hem of the dress. It's favorable for autumn or winter weddings.

- **Chapel**—Longer than the court, brush, and Watteau, this train can run as long as 54 inches from the waist. It's one of the most popular train lengths today, as it's elegant and easy to move beneath.
- **Semi-Cathedral**—Longer than a chapel, but not as long as a cathedral.
- **Cathedral**—Slightly more formal than the chapel, this train extends up to 90 inches from the waist. This train tends to allow for bustle and is oftentimes removable.
- **Royal**—Also referred to as a monarch style, this train is the most dramatic of the options and stretches up to 144 inches from the hem of the gown.

Veils

Lengths and styles of veils include*:

- **Birdcage**—This little veil is meant to fall in front of the face and over the eyes. It pairs well with the blusher.
- **Blusher**—This is the shortest veil and falls even with the chin or the very top of the chest. This is the veil many women wear over their faces and flip back once they're down the aisle. It pairs easily with longer veils.
- **Elbow**—Slightly longer than the blusher, elbow veils fall to about the elbow. They're approximately 25 inches long.
- **Flyaway**—Not particularly formal, this veil falls at about the shoulder, has multiple layers, and provides some fun.
- **Fingertip**—Longer than the elbow but shorter than the cathedral, this style is comfortable and carefree and falls at about 45 inches.

- **Waltz**—Typically 54 inches long, this veil falls at the shin, between the knee and the ankle.
- **Chapel**—This one is also appropriate for formal weddings and typically runs the length of the dress and down to the floor. It's approximately 90 inches long.
- **Cathedral**—This one is more appropriate for formal weddings and typically runs the length of the dress and down to the floor. It's approximately 120 inches long from headpiece to hem.
- **Mantilla**—Held in place with a comb, this veil can be cut to any length and is typically circular or scallop-edged.

***Note:** These measurements in this table are approximates and will vary depending on the height of the bride.

Types of veil bases include:

- **Wire comb**—This base works best if you wear your hair up and plan on placing the veil at the top of your head.
- **Elastic loops**—These loops allow for more flexibility for your hairdressers and work best with buns and updos.
- **Velcro**—Enough said.

To make a veil your own, you may work with someone like Sara Brosious to either embellish an existing or create a custom piece. "When designing a custom headpiece or veil, I work with the bride to recommend a style and length that compliments the dress and overall mood and feel of the wedding," Brosious said.

She continues:

I typically try to match the fabric used for the veil exactly to the dress. Occasionally, it makes sense for the veil to be in a contrasting fabric, serving as a fun statement piece and accent to the gown. . . .

I love taking vintage lace from a relative's gown or matching lace from the bride's actual gown and creating a nice accent headpiece to the dress. It should complement the dress and not take away from the beauty of it or compete with it.

Depending on the style of the dress additional ways to customize the veil can be to add special beading, feathers, ribbon, or silk flowers. I am a fan of the old saying "something old, something new, something borrowed, something blue." I often take a broach or family heirloom jewelry piece and work it into a veil. The possibilities are endless!

Pay Attention!

While you're shopping for veils, pay attention to the details, specifically where they begin and where they end. Are they only on the floor, from the waist down, or do they run from top to bottom? This is important, because some of the details will cost you extra, especially if the entire veil is covered in them. These embellishments may include:

• Appliques	• Fringes
• Beading	• Quilting
• Bows	• Ribbons
• Brains	• Ruffles
• Embroidery	• Sequins

Other Things to Think About

When shopping for your wedding day attire, you may forget to think about the following, which may actually have a big impact!

- **Color**—If you're pale or fair skinned, medium skinned, or have yellow or pink undertones to your skin, don't buy a bright white dress. Ivory, champagne, or blush will work better. If you have dark skin or olive undertones, most shades of white will work beautifully, though you should also consider ivories and champagnes. Consider the traditions and customs of your culture, too. Chinese brides tend to wear red and Indian weddings are a sea of various colors.

- **Sleeves**—So many options for this one! Short sleeves, long sleeves, three quarter-length sleeves, and cap sleeves are the most common and straightforward, but you can also choose Juliette, puff, butterfly, bell, and bishop sleeves.

Pregnant Brides

If you happen to be expecting when you get engaged or when it comes time to start dress shopping, consider purchasing an empire waist or an A-line with a bunch of ruching. You won't know your measurements when you start shopping, so it's best to purchase a dress with a loose waist that you can grow into. If you can find a salon that will work with you, you may be able to delay your purchase a few months—or you can wait until closer to the ceremony and buy a dress off the rack.

- **Jackets**—Another great way to make your dress your own; most jackets can be customized or made out of leftover fabric from your dress. If you're having a winter wedding, this accessory may come in handy.
- **Gloves**—Lace, satin, or one of a kind. Like jackets, these can easily be customized and can add a bit of flare to your wedding day attire.

Should I bring my future spouse dress shopping?

This just depends on your relationship. Some husbands- or wives-to-be want to be involved and others don't. My fiancé asked me not to even show him the styles or dresses I was pinning because he wanted to be entirely surprised the day of our wedding. (He did this with our senior prom, too.)

If you do decide to bring your partner with you when you're dress shopping, just remember to stay true to what *you* want. Don't shop for them; shop for you.

And if you find that having them tag along is stressful, ask them to leave the appointment or schedule a new appointment and ask them to stay home. Explain why. They should try their best to understand.

Dress Shopping

This is the exciting part! By now, you've done your research, you have an idea of what you're looking for, and you've gone crazy on Pinterest. You've also determined your budget and you're ready to start shopping—or at least browsing.

If you're not ready to shop just yet, but you want to look around, feel free to comb the racks without trying anything on. This may be best to do alone if you're comfortable with the idea; when you take an entourage with you, they're going to want to see you try things on. If you're not there yet, go alone. Tell the consultant that you're just browsing, look at what you want, and leave when you're finished. No pressure.

Choose a Team

When you know what you want, approach the people you'd like to go with you. These should be people you trust to tell you the truth about how you look in anything you try on. Although honesty is definitely a requirement here, your entourage also needs to be supportive and needs to understand what you're looking for and how you really want to look on your wedding day.

Your team may consist of your mother, mother-in-law, sister(s), sister-in-law(s), bridesmaids or bridesmen, close friends, grandparents, or your father. Your wedding planner may also be an option, though it may not be a popular one.

Make Appointments

After you choose your team, call at least three dress shops and set up consultations. Ask your friends where they've bought their gowns, search online for stores in the area, and be sure to read the reviews. If you can find a salon with a long-standing reputation and many happy customers, you should be good to go.

Plan to try on dresses at these appointments, but don't plan on committing to one. Tell yourself that you're simply looking and having a good time; don't put the pressure on yourself to make a purchase the first time out. You may try on three dresses, or thirty, but keep your options open until you're absolutely certain you've found the right one. Don't settle!

Just as you would when meeting with vendors, prepare a list of questions to ask the employee at the bridal salons or departments while you're booking your appointment. These may include:

- How long is my appointment?
- Will a specific sales associate be helping me individually?
- On average, how many dresses can bride-to-be's try on in this time period?
- Is there a limit to how many dresses I can try on?
- What should I bring?
- Am I allowed to browse the racks or will the consultant do it for me?
- If I'm allowed, are my guests also allowed?
- What sizes are the samples in your store?
- What is your store's price range?
- What is your return policy?

Once you've made your appointments, be sure to put together a bag to bring with you that will make trying on dresses easier. You may want to do your hair and makeup (not exactly like, but similar to) how you think you may want to wear your hair for your big day—or just so you don't feel frumpy as you try on one beautiful gown after another.

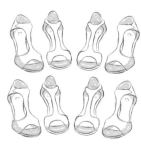

Items you should bring with you to your appointment include:

- A strapless **bra**
- **Panty hose**—If panty hose don't have a control top, bring spanks
- **Shoes**—Make sure the heel is a similar height to the heel you plan on wearing on your wedding day
- Any **accessories** you already own that you *must* wear down the aisle or at the reception (gloves, jewelry, bouquet, props, etc.)
- A **look book**, or a collection of gowns that you've seen and admired and may want to try on. This will give your consultant an idea of which dresses she should pull from the rack.
- Any **hair accessories** you may need in case you want to try different looks (brush, hair ties, pins, headbands, etc.)

It might be kind of obvious, but be sure that when you make your appointment to try on gowns that *you're actually ready to try on gowns.* Put your insecurities to the side and let the consultant dress you up. You'll never find *the* dress if you're afraid to put any on. Even if you're not feeling the most comfortable—maybe you're a little bloated, maybe you have a headache, maybe you have a bit of sunburn on your shoulders—suck it up and follow through with your appointment. Don't waste the sales associate's time or the time of the friends and family members who came with you. If you're not ready for whatever reason, reschedule. But don't wait until last minute. That's just rude.

Connection Matters

If you arrive at your appointment and you don't like the gowns available, do not get along with your consultant, or find that you don't trust the management, leave—do *not* buy your gown from a person or a place you don't trust. Even if buying from this person means saving hundreds of dollars, don't do it. You feel weird for a reason; follow your gut and don't hand over your credit card.

Trying on Gowns

When you arrive at your appointment, you'll discuss what you think you're looking for with the consultant and she will either walk you through the racks or she'll choose a few gowns that she thinks may work while you disrobe.

Although you should stick to your guns about what you want, you also need to be open-minded. Just because you *think* you may look best in a mermaid dress doesn't necessarily mean that you'll walk away with a mermaid dress. Trust your consultant; if she brings back a ball gown and says she thinks it might work for you, try it on. Don't crinkle your nose and shake your head. Just try it on. If you don't like it, you can take it off immediately and no one ever has to know.

When you've tried one on that you're comfortable showing your guests, walk out with your head held high and let them tell you what they see. As you walk, take note of how the dress moves around you. Plus, ask yourself the following questions:

- Is it easy to walk in?
- Can you sit down and stand up without difficulty?
- Will you be able to get in and out of the limo/car?
- Can you dance? Shake it and see.
- What happens when you raise your arms?
- What happens when you bend over?
- Think about all the hugs you're going to give. Will the embellishments get stuck on your guests' clothes?
- Can you breathe?

All of these questions should be answered via a movement test. Reenact certain movements you'll be required to make on your big day and see how the dress reacts. If it's too stiff, too big, too heavy, etc., try on a different one. The last thing you want to be on your wedding day is uncomfortable (or blue in the face).

After you've tried a few on, eliminated the types that don't look right with your frame, and have seen yourself from top to bottom with accessories in place, go back to the one that felt the best—the one that made you feel like a bride. Memorize it, write down the designer, ask the consultant for a quote on the final price based on any embellishments or adjustments you've discussed, ask her to put

it on hold, and let her know when you'll be calling back with your decision. Then leave and go to your other appointments if you've planned them.

If you can't stop thinking about a particular dress or you want to try it on again before a new crowd of people, call the salon and ask for another appointment. Tell them what you're looking to do and see when they can fit you in. If you still love that dress above all other ones that you've tried on—and if you can picture yourself walking down the aisle in it and it truly makes you feel beautiful, inside and out—then that's a wrap. You've found your dress!

If there is *any* doubt in your mind, though, sleep on it for a few more nights. Don't buy a dress just because it's the best one you've seen so far; you wouldn't marry your partner just because he or she was the best option at the time, right? He or she has to be the only option you want; the only person you can't live without. Apply this thinking to your dress.

If you're not ready to commit, make more appointments at other salons, pin a few more gowns in your look book, talk your maid of honor's ear off. Just be sure you don't go too crazy;

you shouldn't try on hundreds of gowns. If you find yourself going down that path and you just can't find what you're looking for, take a break. A few weeks or a month later, try again. (Or ask your bridal party to go on a road trip and see what a nearby city or state has on their racks.)

Remember what this day is about!

Some brides have a hard time with gown shopping—and wedding planning in general—because they don't like to be the center of attention. They don't want everyone looking at them, analyzing them, talking about them. Some brides relish this spotlight, while others would rather the entire day be quick and painless. I considered—and "playfully" suggested on numerous occasions—simply going to the courthouse with my fiancé mostly because of this feeling.

But at the end of the day, you have to realize that everyone who RSVPs yes to your wedding is there to support you and your partner. They want to see you happy; they aren't there to judge you or to make you uncomfortable. They came to celebrate, to have a good time—and that's what you need to focus on: having a good time. Which dress is going to help you have the best time? Pick that one.

Making Your Purchase

You've asked a million questions before getting to this point, and now it's time to ask a million more. Before you hand over the credit card (and *always* pay for your wedding dress with a credit card—it provides the perfect record of purchase and convenience in case something goes wrong!), make sure you ask the following:

- Is a fabric sample available? Check it for feel and color.
- What accessories would look best with this dress? (veils, trains, gloves, etc.)
  - Do they sell those accessories in the salon?
  - Is there a discount for bundling the accessories with the dress?
- Which undergarments are most appropriate to wear with this dress?
- Can I schedule my first appointment for alterations*?
  - How many fittings can I schedule ahead of time?
  - Can they estimate how much the previously discussed alterations will cost?

Note: When you order your dress, be sure you choose a realistic size. Do *not* order down because you *hope* you'll be a certain size by the time of your wedding. If your dress is too big, you can always get it altered. If it's too tight, you may need to add material—which could also add to the cost.

When you offer your credit card for payment, be sure the salon has all relevant information:

- your full name
- your phone number
- the name of the salesperson who helped you
- the date of your wedding
- the size you ordered and other measurements
- estimated cost of the gown
- your list of alterations and their estimated costs
- delivery date of the dress to the salon

Ask them to make you a copy of this information and all receipts for the deposit you've paid so far and the remaining balance on your purchase. Also be sure to ask how many fittings are included in the price (and have them write it down) and get a copy of their cancellation policy.

If all goes according to plan, you should schedule your first fitting approximately six weeks before, your second fitting about a month before, and your final fitting should be one or two weeks before the wedding. Bring all of your accessories to the final fitting so you can see how the entire ensemble will look.

Tip!

When you go back to the store for your fittings, whether it's your first or third, be sure you make the most of your time and always be honest. Try to see it from every angle; consider your seamstress's ideas and listen to what your mother, maid of honor, or bridesmaids think and then figure out what you think.

If you don't like the way your dress looks or feels on you, say something. Be vocal. Don't settle.

Budget Bridal Dresses

As quoted in chapter 3, the average wedding attire cost is approximately $1,600; however, every woman knows at least one other bride who spent more than that (double or even triple) on just their dress. No shoes, no jewelry, no train or veil—just the dress. If you have the money to spend and you want to spend it on a gorgeous, one-of-a-kind gown, that's great!

If your budget is closer to today's average estimation and you're taking the budget-conscious approach to planning your wedding, here's a few tips to help you get what you want while still saving money:

- **Wear family heirlooms**—Perhaps your mother's dress fits and is still in good condition, or your older (or twin!) sister wears the same size and would loan you her dress.
- **Borrow from friends**—Some women aren't sentimental, so a friend may let you either borrow or buy her dress. Maybe one of them bought a dress but decided to wear a different one later and couldn't return the original. Ask around; you never know what you'll find.
- **Rent from stores or boutiques**—Plenty of stores and websites are available today to help brides and bridesmaids rent gowns. Rent the Runway (renttherunway.com), for example, allows brides to rent their dresses for four or eight days, arranges try-ons, and also has accessories such as jackets and jewelry to rent. Depending on the city in which you're shopping, you may find some bridal boutiques and shops that allow for rentals, as well. See page 72 for more.
- **Visit sample sales**—You can find deeply discounted gowns at sample sales hosted by designers, dress salons, and other shops. Most of the time, the discount can be around 75 percent.
- **Keep it simple**—Maybe you don't need the beading or other embellishments. Maybe you don't need a ten-foot

train. If you like the way a more basic style fits your body, buy it and dress it up with borrowed or rented accessories.

- **Make your own**—Plenty of crafty brides (or their sisters, mothers, or friends) enjoy the challenge of making their own gowns. If you want your dress to truly be your own and you have the skills to make it, this option would be perfect for you. Many designers share wedding dress patterns and the bigger the city, the better your fabric options. Take a road trip and chat up salespeople while picking out your fabric. You can typically trust their recommendations.

Alternative Bridal Attire and Accessories

You don't need a white gown to be a bride on your wedding day. In fact, you don't even need the gown! Many of today's brides are opting for different colored fabric, cocktail dresses, and even tuxedos or suits. (The tux doesn't need to be white if you don't want it to be, either!)

If white isn't for you, if tulle isn't for you, if skirts in general aren't for you, don't sweat it. Feel free to buck tradition and try on a bright pink dress, buy a two-piece set, or browse the Internet for lace or satin suits. Do what's best for you. If you're comfortable and happy with what you see when you try on your attire and look in the mirror, then that's all you need.

What will the groom wear?

Similar to brides, grooms can also either purchase or rent their tuxedos or suits. While renting a wedding gown may seem like a new idea to many, renting tuxedos or suits for the groom or the bride who would like to wear a suit isn't anything revolutionary or unexpected.

While shopping for a suit or tux, grooms—regardless of a budget—should try their best not to look cheap. You don't need to put out the money for a designer brand if you don't want to, but you do want to make sure the clothes fit. In addition, you should examine the breathability of the fabric, the feel and sheen, and the weight. Craftsmanship should also be considered. This is your wedding day; save the budget rentals for your first born's prom.

If a suit or tux doesn't fit comfortably or doesn't look quite right, you may need to get it tailored. Be sure your partner doesn't send his or her measurements to the tailor without first being measured, preferably by a professional and not you with measuring tape and guestimates.

When purchasing a tux or suit, discuss everything you would when buying a wedding gown, including scheduling fittings and cancellation policy. When renting, discuss the return plan with the shop you're renting from. Even being a few hours late could cost you a few hundred unbudgeted dollars.

Again, similar to shopping for bridal accessories, make sure your partner figures out tie color and shape, sock color, button covers, and cufflinks well before the big day.

Remember: The groom's decisions in this area will affect his groomsmen, so be sure to keep them updated as decisions are made. While the bride is going to stand out amongst her bridesmaids, the groom's party tends to dress exactly like him and anyone not following his lead will undoubtedly stand out. Unless that's the point, this is something you'll want to avoid.

For information on bridal party attire, see page 127.

7

Wedding Bands

"Affection is responsible for nine-tenths of whatever solid and durable happiness there is in our lives."
—C. S. LEWIS

Your wedding rings may be small in size (and unfortunately easy to lose!) but that doesn't make them any less important than the venue you choose or the first song you dance to. In fact, they are even more important—you'll spend a few hours in your reception hall and will recall fond memories whenever you hear your song, but your wedding ring will be worn daily and will make you think of the person you love and all the reasons you love him or her every time you look at it, day or night.

You should try to purchase your wedding bands no later than three months before your wedding; if you think you're going to get a custom ring made or you want a certain amount of engraving, then you should probably get your order in four or five months before. However, the timing of this purchase isn't set in stone—you can purchase it as early as you'd like. Just make sure you store it somewhere safe!

Keep in mind that if your style is simple, there's nothing wrong with buying a simple band. Don't feel like you need to get something crafty or impressive or expensive. You won't be selling it, so its value is purely sentimental. If, later in your marriage, you want to dress it up, you can add to it or retire it and buy a new one for a milestone anniversary.

Make it a date!

Unlike dress shopping, cake tasting, and most of the other tasks you'll need to check off, shopping for your wedding bands can be something you and your partner do with each other and without distractions, interruptions, or "advice" from anyone else. These are for you and only you, so only your opinions matter.

There are plenty of ways you can make this activity romantic. Perhaps you can dress up, go for a nice, intimate dinner, and then go shopping. Or, after you've chosen your rings, celebrate with a bottle of wine at your favorite wine bar or share dessert.

All that matters is that you're both happy with the rings you choose (and that they fit within your budget, of course).

Do Your Research

Just like dress shopping, you should know a little something about what you're looking for before you get serious. You can browse the glass cases at any jewelers (try a few on, if you

want) or you can spend some time Googling. Take notes, rip pages out of your wedding magazines, and try to narrow down the selection as best as you can. Decide on which shape and style you want—will a simple band do, or do you want to embellish it? Should it be vintage or modern? Does it have to match your engagement ring? Will you go for a custom band or does one exist that you're already in love with?

If you do choose to try a few on, pay attention to how they feel on your finger—if you had to wear it 24/7, is it comfortable?

Note!

If you choose to wear both your engagement and wedding band on the same finger, tradition says to wear your wedding band beneath your engagement ring so it is closer to your heart.

This arrangement also tends to be more comfortable.

But, as I keep stressing, do whatever you want. It's your band and your finger.

Is it too heavy? Do you like the color of the metal against your skin? (Does it make you itchy?)

Metal

If you normally wear jewelry, you most likely already know which type of metal you want to use for your wedding band, as you'll want the band to match the pieces you wear on a day-to-day basis—you may *only* wear silver (or white gold), like me. The majority of brides also like to match the metal of their engagement rings to the metal of their wedding bands. However, if you mix and match your jewelry and you like the look, you could follow that idea for your wedding band, too.

The most common types of metal for wedding bands include:

- **Gold**—yellow, white (with nickel), and rose (with copper) are the three most common golds used for bands. While shopping for a gold band, choose a 14 karat or 18 karat, not 24, as they tend to be extra soft and not as durable.
- **Platinum**—more expensive and certainly more durable than gold, platinum also makes diamonds shine brighter than a gold band will.
- **Palladium**—lighter and less expensive than platinum, this is a white precious metal that is becoming more common for wedding bands.
- **Titanium**—strong, but extremely lightweight, titanium is a great pick if you work with your hands throughout the day. This is typically the top choice for men.

This decision will most likely be difficult for the groom—or the bride who doesn't wear a lot of jewelry—because he doesn't have anything to match. He may be starting from scratch, so he may spend a bit more time on this detail than you will. Be patient with him.

Allergies? Platinum is hypoallergenic. Sensitive skin? Titanium's the way to go.

What if I don't like my engagement ring?

If you haven't yet fallen in love with your engagement ring and your fiancé bought it off the rack and didn't have any customizations done to it, then it may not be too late to return it. Be honest with him or her. If you don't think it looks right on your finger or it's just not your style, speak up. Feelings may hurt, but your partner will most likely bend over backwards to find you something else that you love.

If it's been a while and you've simply fallen out of love with your engagement ring, look into getting a customizable band that can combine your engagement ring into the band in a beautiful, sophisticated way. You may be able to eliminate the parts you don't like and keep the ones you do. Jewelers are talented; tell them what you want and see what they think they can do.

The last option is to not wear your engagement ring once you have your wedding band. Store it somewhere safe and come back to it for special occasions. Distance makes the heart grow fonder, right? Perhaps a few months (or years) of little to no wear will help.

Stones & Gems

Many brides and grooms like to keep their wedding bands simple without any adornments. If your budget allows, though, there's nothing wrong with adding a few stones.

Styles on the Band

The most common styles when you're incorporating stones into your bands are:

- **Bar**—A small bar of metal separates each stone on the band.
- **Channel**—Stones are set between two panels of metal that encase them; think of a river—the bank are the panels and the stones are the water.
- **Gypsy**—Stones are sunk into the band, equidistant from each other, and are flush with the band itself. This style is popular with bands for both the bride and the groom.
- **Infinity**—Stones are placed either bar, channel, or gypsy-style around the entire band. Note that infinity bands may cause problems in the future if you lose or gain a significant amount of weight, as you'll most likely need to cut through a stone to adjust the band.

Types of Stones & Gems

As you already known, diamonds are typically the stones used in wedding bands. However, you don't need to follow that line of thinking if you don't want to. You can include your birthstones or stones that represent your school colors (perhaps that's where you met) or even stones that remind you of specific events or places you've been to together. There's no hard and fast rule about choosing the stones you want in your wedding band; if you can afford them and they're durable, then go for it.

You may find the stones you're looking for at your jeweler, or you may find them somewhere within your family. If your mother or grandmother has a diamond she doesn't wear anymore, for example, you could take it from her ring and add it to yours. If a family member has a broken stone, you can have it reshaped and placed in your band.

If you choose to either wear a complete wedding band passed down within the family, or simply get a ring made with pieces of said band, you may not feel comfortable wearing it on a daily basis. Depending on the age of the metal or stones, it may be extremely valuable—financially or sentimentally. An option here is to get a duplicate made with a less expensive metal or stone to wear daily. In the meantime, you can store your prized possession in a safe place and pull it out for special occasions.

Engravings

Before you purchase a ring—and before you have it sized— speak with your partner about any engravings or inscriptions you want to include on your wedding bands. They don't have to match, and one of you can get one and not the other. You should know exactly what you want the inscription to be before you start shopping, though. Adding it later, when the ring is purchased and sized, will be frustrating and potentially impossible. When you're shopping, you should tell the jeweler what you want the engraving to be and see if it's something he feels he can fit in the ring.

Engraving and inscriptions could be symbols that mean something to you both, the date of your wedding or engagement or dating anniversary, your initials, your names, nicknames, an important phrase or song lyric, etc. The only limitation placed on this is the actual size of your ring. And, similar to infinity bands, you want to make sure the engraving doesn't go around the entire band, as it may need to be cut to adjust for size later on.

Ring Shopping

When shopping for your wedding bands, the same rules apply that we discussed for shopping for your wedding dress. You need to do the research and have an idea of what you want so you don't get overwhelmed when stepping into the jewelers. Once you both (if you're both wearing a band) have an idea of what you want, then it's time to start shopping. Where can you go to buy a wedding band?

First, if you have an engagement ring that you love, visit the jeweler where that ring was purchased. Show the jeweler your ring and ask if your engagement ring was part of a set—there's a chance a wedding band exists that will pair perfectly with your engagement ring. If it is not part of a pair, ask if there would be some type of discount available for purchasing your band at the same place as your engagement ring. Sometimes loyalty really matters!

If you don't have an engagement ring or you're unimpressed by the jeweler's collection, then move on to another store. You can go to major jewelers who sell wedding rings, such as Jared, Kay, or Zales. You could also visit department store jewelry

departments such as Macy's. Another option is shopping online via Amazon or Overstock, but then you run the risk of not loving what you purchased because you couldn't try it on (and also being extremely anxious when it's shipping!).

Some brides and grooms may be looking for something more unique, perhaps not something you pick out of a catalog or something already designed and placed in a glass case. If you want a wedding band that is truly you, then consider visiting a smaller, local jeweler or jewelry artist. If you really like the style of a designer's jewelry, but they either don't have wedding bands on display or it seems like they may not design them, don't be afraid to ask them if they'd consider making you one. They may be flattered and may also enjoy the challenge. In this case, you will have a truly one-of-a-kind ring.

No matter where you're shopping, remember that you don't need to purchase your band from someone you don't trust. Even if you've been sized and you've just spent three hours discussing bar versus channel settings, if you don't feel like you and the jeweler are on the same page—or if anything at all doesn't feel *right*—then you can walk away. This is your wedding ring; you will wear this ring every day for the rest of your life. Do. Not. Settle.

Questions to Ask Your Jeweler

Before you pay, you're going to want to ask the jeweler questions, such as the following:

- If we bring in the stones to place within the band, is there is any type of discount?

- How much is due right now?
- What is the payment schedule like?
- When will our rings be available to try on?
- When can I pick them up to take home?
- Do you have a return policy?
- Do you recommend a specific type of insurance?
- What happens if one or both of us loses our rings?
- How can we care for our rings?
    - How can we spot loose stones or buff our marks on the metal or stone?
    - If we came back for a checkup once a year (cleaning and making sure the stones are in good shape), is there a charge?

Again, if you don't feel like the jeweler is being honest with you or you don't feel their schedule can work with yours, keep the plastic in your purse and move on to another jeweler. There are plenty of places to try.

Do our rings need to match?

Absolutely not!

You are two different people, and even though you may have similar interests, that doesn't mean you share the same style. Your partner may enjoy yellow gold and you may have previously sworn to only ever wear white gold. You may want a little (or a lot of) glitz and your future spouse may not want any. If you're set on having your bands match in some way, consider getting matching or complementary inscriptions.

The Ugly Truth about Your Wedding Rings

Diamond mining negatively affects the environment and the earth. The process of removing them from riverbeds, for example, upsets an entire ecosystem—all the plants and animals that live in that river are disrupted by miners hunting for these precious gems. In addition, when all is said and done, those miners see very little (if any) money for their time.

The same holds true for those who mine for the gold used in our wedding bands. The chemicals they use to extract the metal from its surrounding rocks are harmful to not only the miners, but also the environment in which they're mining. In recent years, gold has become so scarce that it's estimated we toss aside thirty tons of waste rock for enough gold to make a single wedding band.

Unfortunately, gold and gemstones are finite materials. This means only a certain number of these materials exists on Earth for our discovery. Once we mine the last of it, it's gone for good.

If you're the environmentally concerned type, you'll most likely want to look into using recycled gold and metals and synthetic stones in your wedding band (and future jewelry purchases). These are not cheaper, less durable, or less attractive options; in fact, many jewelers have difficulty telling the difference between a "real" gemstone and synthetic one.

Caring for Your Ring

First, make sure you buy a metal and a stone setting that is durable; consider what your hands go through on a day-to-day basis and purchase your ring accordingly. You should clean your ring regularly, as body oils tend to build up on, around, and in it. As noted, when you're shopping for and purchasing your ring, ask the jeweler for advice on caring for your ring. They will most likely tell you to have the following on hand for cleaning:

- Chamois cloth (for shining)
- Dish soap
- Warm water
- Soft-bristled toothbrush
- Cloth or towel (lint-free)

The type of metal and gemstone in your rings will depend on how you clean them. Some stones can be soaked in a bowl of warm water and dish soap, while others can stand up to ammonia-based cleaners. If you're using a toothbrush to scrub your ring, be sure to get in the crevices—like your teeth, you really need to get in there; don't just brush the surface!

When you're cleaning, be gentle and look for loose prongs, scratches, and any oddities. According to wedding planner Mindy Weiss, one trick to tell if you have a loose stone is to hold it close to your ear and shake your hand. If you hear any type of rattling, something's wrong. If you think your ring is in bad shape, bring it to your jeweler for an inspection and repair. Though they will often take a look at it and even clean it free of charge, expect to pay for repairs.

In addition to cleaning your ring, you should store it properly. Don't throw it in your jewelry box with other pieces; it can scratch if it hits a hard piece the wrong way.

When you purchase your rings, you may be offered an insurance policy. Discuss this with your partner and decide whether this is important to you. Sometimes your home owner's policy will include jewelry, but this is not always the case. You may need to get a jewelry policy to cover your rings, and this type of insurance may require annual checkups and appraisals every few years. Just another reason to keep your rings in good shape!

Wedding Band Alternatives

If you feel like breaking tradition, there are plenty of ways to do so in this area!

Switch fingers

Let's say your engagement ring is oddly shaped and doesn't pair well with traditional wedding bands. Or, let's say you've decided you don't want your engagement ring and wedding band to match. You don't need to wear both of these on the same finger if you don't have to. Hell, you don't even have to wear them on the same hand.

If you're going to take this route, be sure you switch your engagement ring to a finger on which your ring will fit. You may need to get it resized, as our hands and fingers are not often the same size.

Engage!

Maybe your engagement (or even your elopement!) was a spur of the moment kind of thing. Maybe there wasn't a ring, but now that you're planning a more formal event, you want a more formal piece of jewelry. If you don't have a diamond on your finger (or whatever stone of your choosing) and you want one, get one! You don't need to buy a wedding band—let your engagement ring act as your wedding ring. And in a few years, should you renew your vows or celebrate a special anniversary, you can explore the option of adding a band to the mix.

Accessorize

One or both of you may use your hands quite a bit, which would expose your rings to harmful chemicals or really disgusting materials (think: fish guts, chicken fat, mud and dirt, or chalk). Certain professions or hobbies may also put your ring at risk—either at risk of being damaged or even being lost.

If this is the case, you can consider placing your wedding band in a bracelet (chain links, leather, cloth, etc.) or wearing it on a chain as a necklace.

Tattoos and Piercings

Wedding band tattoos are a thing! If jewelry isn't for you, but you want to show each other that your presence in each other's lives is permanent, here's your best option.

You can get them in any color, any shape, any style. They can be as big or as small as you want. They can match or they don't have to. They can incorporate symbols, letters, numbers, phrases . . . And you'll never lose them! The possibilities are limited by the amount of skin your have on your finger and your budget. And that's it!

In fact, if you want to add a gemstone to your tattooed wedding band to dress it up, you can! Microdermal piercings involve embedding the stone of your choice into your skin. You can do this on your finger, right in the middle of your inked band, or you can place it somewhere nearby. A popular place is the webbing between your thumb and your pointer. Please note, though, that this could be painful and that you'll still need to be careful—microdermal piercings can get caught on just about anything, and getting them ripped out of your body can't be all that much fun.

Ring Stories

"I got my wife's engagement ring locally, a flexible, woven band, made in India. Gold prices were sky-high, so I held off on mine. I wore a black rubber washer as my wedding band. A friend told his girlfriend, 'I'm getting one of those. Did you see? F—ing *onyx*.' We went to India on honeymoon, so I ended up getting my wedding band there. But it's not easy to get to a gold shop. Every rickshaw driver we met wanted to take us to *his* friend's shop, so we got out of seven rickshaws and finally walked. At the end of the day, gold was half-price over there—still crazy inflated, but yellow and heavy. And prettier than rubber. Mine is a plain, One Ring to Rule Them All style band. Hers flexes when you push it. But both are Indian gold, and they only do high karat. And her actual wedding band is so thin we've already had it mended. Mine is chonky. So the style is very different, color the same." —GABRIEL S. (@gabrielsquailia)

"We both have silver bands but mine has diamonds in it. We went shopping together." —JOCELYN G.

"He chose my engagement ring and we went to Bartikowsky's to have my wedding band designed to match it. It's five sapphires that match my diamond to represent blue and white for Penn State University since that is where we met. The jeweler had to make two because the first one didn't fit snuggly against my other ring. His band is white gold and does not match mine." —ANGELA H.

"My engagement ring is an heirloom that's been in my husband's family so long no one quite remembers which generation originally bought it. Jewelers have told me the particular way the diamond is cut hasn't been common since the nineteenth century." —SARAH C.

"We designed my engagement ring—it's a round diamond we stole out of a family heirloom, and it's set in a ring with two sapphires and filigree. My wedding band is white gold with my great grandmother's diamonds— European cut, which they don't do anymore—and sapphires. Sam's ring is tungsten but doesn't match mine other than it's also silver-toned." —JESS L.

"We wanted simple, and I thought I didn't care that much, so I just went down to the 'district' and got simple thin bands (I especially don't love those chunky bands on men, and I thought I was too low maintenance for a diamond band)—platinum for me, gold for him, inscribed with the date inside. Within a year, I regretted my quick choice. It was too thin, and disappeared behind my engagement ring (solitaire). So for our fifth anniversary, Andy said I should go get myself one I liked (romantic, right?). I went to Tiffany for ideas, decided on one that had tiny diamonds half-way around (the lady there said not to get stones all around because after you have babies, you're going to want to have it resized—she was right! I totally did). I had one made just like it at a local jeweler (much cheaper than Tiffany!) and I was happy. Still wear it, and we're having our fifteenth this year." —NATASHA S.

8

The Parties—
The People and the Places

"You come to love not by finding the perfect person, but by
seeing an imperfect person perfectly."
—SAM KEEN

• • •

*M*any excited brides and grooms don't heed the advice given
in chapters 1 and 2 and jump right into their planning.
One of the first things they do is promise away their wedding
party slots. Around the same time, they may also be throwing
together an engagement party with encouragement from
friends and family so everyone can celebrate ASAP. Ideas may
be flying for the bridal shower and bachelor and bachelorette
parties and it could get overwhelming—fast.

These elements—including selecting your wedding party—
all require more than a little thought and the timing has to be

just right for each. Although the rules aren't as exact as booking your venue, planning a menu, or selecting your wedding dress, there's still quite a bit to consider and keep in mind.

Selecting Your Wedding Party

Today, the roles others play in your wedding are more about support and representation of you and your partner than the tasks they'll actually handle or help you with. Note that you absolutely don't need a wedding party if you don't want one—if you just want the two of you up front at the ceremony and seated at a sweetheart table at the reception, then that's what you should do. However, if you don't want to buck tradition in this area, you will most likely be asking your friends and family to take part as bridesmaids, bridesmen, groomsmen, groomswomen, flower girl(s), and ring bearer(s).

Don't Stress Over Equal Numbers

Symmetry may be a beautiful thing, but it's not necessary for a wedding. If you want to have an equal number of bridesmaids and groomsmen on each side, you can, but don't feel like you have to. If you're concerned that it may look a bit lopsided during the ceremony, ask a few to swap sides.

In 2015, one bride broke the Guinness Word Record for most bridesmaids in a single wedding when she asked 168 women to stand up for her at her wedding in Safety Harbor, Florida. Her groom did not, however, have 168 groomsmen.

Traits

The men and women you choose to stand up for you on your wedding day should be responsible, punctual, supportive, honest, and able to play well with others. Ideally, they should know you well and should know what you want and why you want it. You want them to tell you what they really  think, in a respectful way, and you also want to know that they're going to fulfill their duties and not be late to your ceremony!

Above all, though, these people should be supportive of your relationship. They should love the idea of the two of you together forever. They should be ecstatic when you tell them you're getting married and they should be more than happy to help, even before they're selected to be a main part of it.

Traits that aren't necessary, but may be helpful, in your wedding party participants include having the money to be part of your big day (again, not an absolute!) and being generally fun to be around.

The people you choose should be those you trust to give you sound advice in a respectful way. They should be open to compromise (the more people involved, the more compromise  will need to occur) and should be communicative with not only you and your partner, but also everyone else in the group. They should be dependable and have a good follow-through track record. If you ask one of your bridesmaids to call and confirm the manicure and pedicure appointments,

When Opinions and Emotions Get in the Way

One of the reasons it's so important to think long and hard before making this decision is that being a bridesmaid can take a toll on a woman—not to mention, on the other members of the bridal party and you. If your potential bridesmaid (or groomsman) is very opinionated, angers easily, and tends to hold grudges, you may not want to ask them to be part of your day. If you often have to listen to all the dramatic situations she finds herself in the middle of, or you can list on more than one hand the people she isn't speaking to at the moment because of this or that, you know what you have to do.

If you ask her anyway, be prepared for battle. Hopefully she'll remember this is your day and that her opinion is not the only one that counts. However, if she's starting fights with the other bridal party members, she's skipping bridal party meetings, she's voiced her disgust for the dress/accessories you chose for her to wear, or she's not being respectful to you or your partner, you may need to fire her.

This can be a very awkward situation, and the best thing to do is to handle it as maturely as possible. Ask to speak to her in private (never gang up on her with the rest of the party!) and in person (no texts!) and tell her you can tell she's unhappy with some of the decisions you've made. Tell her that you feel she's making the wedding planning more difficult than it needs to be. Let her tell you why she's behaving this way or saying the things she is. Maybe it's a bigger problem than her simply hating the color orange or not liking the groomsman she'll be walking down the aisle with. Maybe she's over budget and she can't afford to be in the wedding anymore. Maybe she's regretting saying yes. Through this conversation, you'll both realize whether she should stay or go.

you have to be able to trust that she'll do it. If you asked a groomsman to get in touch with the DJ and ask if he has a specific song in his collection, then, again, you need to know he'll do it without you needing to remind or nag him.

To ask or not to ask, that is the question.

The men and women you choose to stand up for you at your wedding should meet the aforementioned qualities. They should be the people you get along with the best, who you trust and can depend on. You should feel comfortable around them and should be confident they won't cause any problems along the way. If you think there's going to be an issue, don't ask them.

Who else should you not ask? Anyone you feel obligated to. You don't need to ask the guys and girls who have previously asked you to be in their weddings. You don't need to ask your sister or brother if you're not close with them. You also don't need to ask your future spouse's siblings if you don't feel a bond with them. This is why it's so important not to promise these

If you feel like someone may be expecting to be asked, and you don't plan on asking them, should you let them know?

That's entirely up to you. It will be an awkward conversation, and many men and women won't bring it up because of that very reason so you don't have to have it. However, if you feel like you need to say something, don't make it personal. Please—please—don't tell someone, "I didn't think you'd get along with my sister" or "I thought you'd be too difficult to shop with" unless you not only don't want them to attend your wedding, but also want them to stop talking to you in general. Instead, tell them the bridal party is family only if that's the case, or that you wanted the numbers to be equal on each side. Come up with something based in fact—make sure it's not a lie. Don't tell her you decided less is more and then have eighteen people up there with you. And don't apologize for your decision.

spots away the second after you get engaged; otherwise, you may assign a spot to a cousin you don't really know that was really meant for your best friend from college.

Don't allow yourself to feel limited with who you can ask to stand with you—mixed wedding parties are perfectly acceptable, and encouraged! You can have bridesmen and bridesmaids. You can have groomsmen and groomswomen. If your groom's sister is his best friend, then she should stand on his side, not yours. So what if she's the only female over there? Who cares?

Also don't feel limited by distance or money. If you have someone in mind who is in eighteen other weddings this year and doesn't live locally, but you've always wanted her to be part of your day, ask her anyway. Tell her she's not obligated, but you wanted to make sure she knew you were thinking of her. She can say no—and she should if she can't afford the dress, the gift, or the travel. If she's out of the country and can't get the time off from work or can't afford the international flight, ask if she wants to Skype or FaceTime during bridesmaid meetings and the ceremony. It may be a little quirky, but, again, so what? At least she's there.

Another group of people not to avoid? Your pregnant friends! She may have a harder time committing to a dress size because she may not know what her size will be around the time of your wedding, but if she wants to be part of the action—and you want her there, of course—then ask! She can say no if she's uncomfortable with the idea or would rather save the money for her diaper fund.

What if they say no?

If you ask someone to be part of your day and they say no, for whatever reason, accept their answer and don't pressure them into reconsidering. Don't make them feel guilty, don't make them feel obligated. Tell them you understand and make sure they know to expect an invitation to the wedding. And then move on. You wouldn't want that one person you didn't ask to be in your wedding to badger you about not being in it, right?

Maid/Matron of Honor and Best Man

This will most likely be the easiest decision you make during your entire planning process. You already know—and have most likely already asked—someone to fill this role, so details here are unnecessary. Like the others, make sure these people are trustworthy and dependable and support your relationship with your future spouse.

If you're having a hard time choosing between your best friend and your sister, for example, it's important to realize that you can have more than one maid/matron of honor and best man. If you have twin sisters or twin brothers, ask them to share the responsibilities. If you have a large bridal party or you have a large budget and are planning an elaborate wedding, you may need the extra hands.

Other Fun Titles for Your Wedding Party As Seen on Buzzfeed

- Bridal Brigade
- Friends of Honor
- Pillars of Strength
- Partners in Crime
- Wedding Squad
- Matrimony Homies

Ring Bearers and Flower Girls

You always need to be a little careful if you're going to have children in your wedding. Many wedding planners suggest that children should be older and mature enough to follow directions and stay focused during the ceremony—especially the long ones. If they're going to walk down the aisle themselves and be expected to behave, then they should be at least six years old.

If you're going to ask younger children, consider having their parents or one of the bridesmaids or groomsmen escort them down the aisle. Once flowers have been dropped or the rings have been handed over, the children can sit with their parents rather than stand up front with the rest.

Note: The ring bearer, in most cases, will not be given the actual rings to carry. These bands, as you know by now, are quite expensive and children aren't always responsible with valuable items. You can give this little guy fake rings or something else to symbolize the rings that he can carry down the aisle (and promptly drop, lose, or shove up his nose).

Four-Legged Friends

Many couples adopt pets together before they get married, and those pets are just as big a part of the family as the flower girls, ring bearers, and even best men. Actually, in some weddings, the pets may even fill those roles!

If you have a dog, cat, ferret, turtle, or any other type of animal in your wedding, it's important to keep them on a leash so they don't wander off during the ceremony. It's also a good idea to make sure they're comfortable with the person walking them down the aisle and sitting with them during the ceremony. Don't hand them over to stranger.

Additional Roles

If you want a few others to be involved (perhaps teenage cousins or siblings ten years your senior or a friend who you became surprisingly close with in recent weeks), you can ask them to be ushers, pass out programs, blow bubbles/throw rice, or greet guests at the reception. You can ask them to help by handing out favors or volunteering to take photos of tables/groups throughout the reception or share/post on social media throughout the night. This isn't as flattering of a request as being a bridesmaid or groomsmen, but they may still be honored to be part of it all.

Group Bonding

Once you have asked your friends and family members to be part of your day, get them together so they can all meet each other if they haven't already. This can be dinner, drinks, lunch, or brunch—anyone who is local should show up and listen to what you have planned and what you need help with.

Have these meetings often throughout the planning process and make sure to keep your bridesmaids and groomsmen

informed of all the decisions you're making so they're fully up to date. If anyone is out of town or can't make it, have them call or Skype in so they can be part of the conversation. If it's just bad timing, send an email after the meeting so anyone missing is informed.

The more time you spend together, the easier it'll be to plan and work together. Everyone will be more likely to be on the same page. When it comes time to do things like dress shop and stuff envelopes, a sense of comradery will outweigh color choice or sleeve style.

Dressing their Best

Choosing wedding party attire can be challenging—so many personal shapes and styles, likes and dislikes, to consider, and so many opinions to weigh. Oftentimes, this topic sparks controversy and angry discussion among bridal party crowds. It's important to discuss with your spouse what colors, styles, etc. you want before going shopping with your crew. This way, you'll already have made some of your decisions and you'll know what you're looking for.

Remember—this is your day, and you may not be able to make everyone happy with your choices. However, if you've chosen the right type of people to stand with you, they'll care more that you like their attire than they do.

Don't forget to budget.

In 2015, the average amount of money bridesmaids spent per wedding was $1,700. Keep this in mind while you're shopping for dresses, planning your bachelorette getaway, and choosing accessories for the big day. Do whatever you can to minimize the damage to your friends' bank accounts.

Ladies' Attire

Shopping for the ladies in your wedding party is most likely going to be more difficult than shopping for the men. This is expected, and it's okay. Share your decisions with your bridesmaids and groomswomen when you've made them and then ask for their ideas. Be sure to be clear that you won't budge on something like color, for example. Feel free to set up a Pinterest page and ask them to pin the styles they're looking for. Create a budget that works for each of you, find out who will be comfortable in which styles and, once you have an idea of what each woman will be wearing, go shopping.

To consider:

- Will all women wear the same dress? The same style, same color?
- Will each woman be allowed to pick the style they feel best suits their bodies?
- Will each woman be allowed to pick a different shade of the color you've chosen?
- Will any of the women be wearing suits? And if so, will they match the men's suits?
- Will your maid/matron of honor wear the same dress as the other women? Or will she get one that differs in style, color, length, etc.?
- Will each woman have their hair done in identical styles? Will they wear identical shoes? Jewelry?
- Should women standing on the groom's side wear the same dress as the bridesmaids? Or should they do something different?

Most of what we discussed in chapter 6 can be applied to bridesmaid dress shopping. Turn back to pages 92 to 101 for a refresher.

Gentlemen's Attire

Depending on the formality of your wedding, the men in your wedding party may need to rent tuxes, purchase (or rent) suits, or find a nice pair of khakis (or jeans!). Be sure your guys know what they should be wearing a few months before they're going to need to have it, just in case they need to get alterations.

To consider:

- Will each man wear the same tux/suit?
- Will each man need a jacket?
- Will each man's tie match? Pocket square? Cuff links? Shoes?
- Should the best man wear the same getup as the groomsmen or should his attire differ in some way?
- Should men standing on the bride's side be dressed identically to the groomsmen?

Flower Girl, Ring Bearer, and Mom

The flower girl's dress will traditionally be white, though some brides may want the flower girl to wear the same color as the bridesmaids in some way, whether through a sash or details on the dress itself. The ring bearer should dress similarly to the groomsmen. If this is important to you, check in with parents' of the children in your wedding to see if they want you to be involved in shopping for these items. They may have it handled, though some would probably appreciate the help!

Who would definitely appreciate your help? Mom!

Shopping for the mother-of-the-bride (or groom) dress is a chance to spend one-on-one time with your mother during what is most likely a crazy time. If she's been writing emails and making phone calls and is as deep into your wedding planning as you are, then she deserves to have your full attention for a few hours.

Spend some time researching the type of dress she thinks would suit her best and then hit the boutiques. Be constructive, be polite, be respectful, and be honest. If you wanted her to help you choose the dress that would make you look and feel your best, then you should return the favor and do the same for her.

The Parties

Once the engagement party is out of the way (for more information on this, see page 9), you'll spend some time interviewing wedding planners, searching for venues and vendors, pinning your favorite do-it-yourself projects, and writing and rewriting your guest list. You'll choose your bridal party, figure out your theme, and then the time will come to start planning all the other smaller celebrations that surround your big day.

Bridal Shower

Luckily, your bridal shower isn't exactly one of the parties you have to plan every detail for, so you can relax a bit during this process. Instead, someone will volunteer to host it and plan it in your honor, and all you really have to is provide a bit of information, show up, and open presents.

The point of the bridal shower is to shower the new couple with items they can use in their new life together. (This is where your registry comes in, as the registry is referred to in the bridal shower invitations and *never* in the wedding invitations. For more information on registering, see page 104.) Although you may feel weird expecting gifts, this is one of those times where you should put those feelings aside and simply get ready to accept what is given to you.

Your bridal shower should take place two to three months before your wedding, and invitations should be sent out two months before the shower itself. Traditionally, your maid/matron of honor will host the event with help from your bridal party; however, oftentimes the mother of the bride, in combination with the mother of the groom, may throw the party instead.

Can I have multiple showers?

You don't have to have just one! Brides who moved away from their hometown and their families may choose to have a bridal shower in their current city of residence for their local friends and coworkers to attend and another at home for their older friends and family to attend. This way no one needs to travel. Brides who have lived in multiple cities may go back to have small showers—perhaps lunches or teas—with their friends in each city. These smaller celebrations will most likely be organized by you; don't expect a host to pop up in every city you've ever lived.

Your host will ask you for a guest list so she can send out the invitations to the shower she is planning. People on your bridal shower list should only be close friends and close family; don't invite every female you plan on inviting to your wedding, especially if they won't know anyone else at the party. However, be sure that everyone you do invite to your shower is definitely invited to your wedding to avoid an awkward conversation later.

Developing the guest list will also require you to decide if your shower will be co-ed or women-only. Co-ed showers are becoming more common and often take place at night with cocktails or an open bar, whereas women-only showers tend to take place in the afternoon and don't typically have any alcohol.

Once you decide who will be in attendance, you're pretty much off the hook! The host and the women helping her will most likely plan some games, decorate the space, and handle the RSVPs. They'll also record the gifts as you open them in front of your guests.

Bachelor and Bachelorette Parties

Bachelor and bachelorette parties are two more parties you don't have to plan! However, again, you are going to have to provide your host (most likely the maid/matron of honor and the best man) with vital information, such as who you want to invite, what you want to do, and what you definitely don't want to do. Although the planning may be out of your hands for these, you still need to be vocal about anything that will definitely ruin your night. If strippers and/or heavy drinking make you uncomfortable, say so. Your host should respectfully avoid those.

Deal with it!
I really hate the spotlight. Do I need to open my gifts at the shower?

Believe me, I can relate. But unfortunately, yes, you do. It's actually considered rude to take all your gifts home and open them yourself. You can do this with your wedding gifts, but you're expected to open all your gifts at your shower, since the party truly is about gift-giving and receiving.

What if I really don't like or need a gift I open?

Slap a smile on your face and say something like, "I can't wait to show this to [spouse]!" or "I know exactly where this will go!" And then move on to the next one.

What if I don't like the theme? Or the décor?

Too bad. Your host put a ton of effort into this party, and you should appreciate it, even if you don't like the centerpieces or the games or the location. Thank her profusely, and while you're sending out thank-you notes for all the shower attendants, be sure to send your host a gift to thank her, as well.

As stated time and time again throughout this book, don't be afraid to buck tradition. If you want to take control of your bachelorette party, do it! Plan the entire trip, weekend, night—whatever it is. If this will ensure that you're going to have a good time, then there's no reason you shouldn't do it.

A lot of brides and grooms feel pressure to go crazy during these parties; if this isn't your scene, don't let your group force it on you. If you would rather go to a nice restaurant, order a tasting menu, and pair it with wine with four of your closest friends, then that's what you should do. If you want to go to a club, order bottle service, and dance until the sun comes up, then go for it.

Bachelor and bachelorette parties should be four to six weeks before the wedding if you're gathering a group to travel to somewhere such as Las Vegas. If you're staying local, it may be two or three weeks before your wedding. If it's small and low-key, no traveling involved, it may take place the week of or the night before your wedding.

Regardless of what you decide to do, you shouldn't be paying for your own drinks or food when you're out for your bachelorette party, so don't feel guilty when the others tell you to put your card away or stuff your cash back into your purse.

Joint Bachelor and Bachelorette Parties

Is this a thing? It is, though not many couples embrace it. If you're truly marrying your best friend and you think having him or her around for the night would make it more fun and exciting, then invite your future spouse and his or her friends if you want to. Or, your groups can come together at some point during the night.

Rehearsal Dinner

The rehearsal dinner takes place after the final ceremony rehearsal and is typically held at a location near your ceremony or reception space (basically, near where the majority of your guests are staying for the celebration). Your wedding party, immediate family, and anyone else actually involved in the wedding (all those who attended the practice) should be invited to this dinner. These invites should be placed within the wedding invitation itself (for more information on invitations, see page 148).

Once you've booked your venue, you should look nearby for your rehearsal dinner space. Decide first whether you simply want a sit-down dinner in a restaurant or if you want to book a larger hall with music or at least room for standing and socializing. Once you find a spot, think about its décor and whether you want to bring in a few decorations. The type of place you choose and its natural ambiance will determine dress code.

Plenty of wedding guests claim that the rehearsal dinner is often their favorite night of wedding weekends. This may be because of all the post-practice excitement in the air or it may be because this party is oftentimes more relaxed and less stressful than the wedding itself.

Note that the groom's family typically pays for the rehearsal dinner and the bride's family typically organizes it, but feel free to mix things up.

After-Party

You may only have your reception venue until 10 or 11 p.m., and maybe that's long enough for some people, but many are in this night for the long haul, and it's up to you to plan to keep them entertained. Find an after-party space that's near to reception site—it'd be fantastic if it was either on the land itself or was within walking distance since most attendees have probably already been drinking for a few hours.

You should book the after-party space at the same time you book the rehearsal dinner space. (Maybe both parties are even at the same location.) Be sure the space has an open bar as well as food, as your guests will be craving a midnight snack and will also most likely want to keep drinking. Also make sure the space is big enough; technically, everyone who attends the wedding is invited to the after party. Not everyone will attend, but you still need to make sure you have the room.

Don't worry about themes or colors or centerpieces for the after-party. You also don't need to send out invitations. Spread the word at the reception and just wait and see who shows up.

And by the way, it's up to you if you want to change out of your wedding attire before heading to your after party. If you're done with your dress or are afraid to get it dirty or stained, change into your yoga pants, throw on a T-shirt or hoodie that says BRIDE or MRS on it (you're bound to have four or five of these at this point) and party comfortably!

Brunch

A post-wedding brunch is not necessary, but it's a nice way to show your immediate family, wedding party, and out-of-town guests how much you appreciate them. The bride's family traditionally pays for this last gathering, but if you and your (now) spouse have the funds, it'd be a nice gesture to pay for it yourself.

Look for your brunch location when you're booking your after-party and rehearsal dinner. Again, it should be close to where all of your out-of-town guests are staying so they don't have to travel much farther. Put the invitation to brunch in your wedding invitations and make sure you get an approximate head count and update your reservation as this changes.

All you really have to decide is whether you want a cocktail brunch or a traditional menu. Then let the caterer or restaurant provide the rest. Enjoy this time with your friends, family, and your new husband or wife!

9

The Devil's in the Details

"What I find about wedding plans is that everyone wants to talk about them when I don't. As soon as I do feel like talking about my wedding plans, their eyes glaze over and I can see them wishing they were dead."
—SUZANNE FINNAMORE, *Otherwise Engaged*

• • •

So, all the big stuff is booked, you know who will be standing by your side, and you're ready to pour some wine and relax, right?

Well, you may feel that way—and you may *really* want that wine—but unfortunately (or fortunately, if you're loving the entire planning process), there's still quite a bit to do!

In this chapter, we'll discuss everything from finalizing your guest list to the do's and don'ts of gift baskets to writing your vows and even thinking ahead to your honeymoon. You can buy entire books and scour the Internet to find out more about each of these subjects, so we'll just cover the basics here. If you're feeling overwhelmed, turn to your wedding planner, your parents, your in-laws, and your bridesmaids and groomsmen for help. With guidance and some organization, they can handle a lot of what you can't.

Finalize the Guest List

By now, you've booked your venues and have hired a caterer and you're aware of your budget, which means you know both the minimum and maximum number of people you can invite to your ceremony and your reception. Early on, you most likely made a rough list of who you were thinking of inviting and that probably led you to the perfect venue. It's time to dig that out.

Depending on how much time has passed since you made your original list, you may be able to remove a few names (maybe you haven't spoken to a friend from college in two years, maybe some of the more senior family members have sadly passed away) and add others (new friends, old friends' new plus ones).

Before you put pen to paper (or send a list off to your invitation designer), consider the following:

- **Plus ones**—Are they invited? Can everyone bring one or only some guests?

- **Children**—Are they invited? And if so, will a children's menu be available and is each meal full-price? Will there be a place for them to gather and play? Is the venue child-appropriate?
- **Work friends**—Should you invite your closest colleagues? Your bosses or supervisors? Is your office or department small enough to invite everyone you work with? If your boss has granted you extra time off to get married or go on your honeymoon, you may want to send an invitation even if you're not incredibly close with him or her.
- **Guaranteed NOs**—Never assume there will be some. Even if you're friends with someone who frequently talks about how much she hates weddings and the idea of marriage as a whole, don't expect her to decline your invitation. She may change her tune within six months and want to party with you!
- **Extended family**—How far is too far? Second cousins? Third? And what about their kids? If you have never met them, don't exchange holiday cards, and couldn't pick them out of a crowd, skip them. And don't get angry when they don't invite you to theirs.

If your parents have been heavily involved in your planning, the most difficult part of finalizing your guest list will most likely be accommodating their requests. If your mother can't imagine the day passing without Aunt Mary's sister-in-law's cousin's kid, spend some time speaking to her. Do you know this person? Will her presence affect your day in any way? Will including her mean you have to leave someone off your priority list? This is your wedding, and you should have final say of the guest list. . . .

However, if your parents have contributed generously to your day, you should really keep their requests in mind and, if you can't accommodate them, respectfully let them know why. Going into the final list, consider blocking off 10 to 20 percent of the list for their priority invites.

Verbal Invites—A Big No

Try as hard as you can to avoid inviting people verbally. When talking about your wedding, don't ask them if they want to attend and don't promise them an invite. In addition, don't ask them for their address and then never send anything. All of these are forms of commitment, and as your date approaches (and everyone will know what that date is, thanks to social media), they'll be waiting for their invitations, regardless of whether their names appear on your final guest list.

The Boss

As previously stated, you should invite your boss if you see him or her on a day-to-day basis and/or if he or she has given you additional time off work while you've run to wedding-related appointments or for your honeymoon. If you work for a bigger company and don't have access to or interaction with your boss, you don't need to invite him or her; however, you may consider inviting your direct supervisor or your department head.

Should you give your boss a plus one? Probably. This will distract him or her from your colleagues, who will be nervous enough drinking and dancing while he or she is close by. Etiquette experts state that bosses typically leaves their employees' weddings after the cutting of the cake, which is usually before everyone has too much to drink and the congo line starts.

Save the Dates and Invitations

Once you have your guest list ready, it's time to decide whether you're going to send Save the Dates to everyone, to some people, or not at all.

If you plan on sending Save the Dates in addition to traditional invitations, you're most likely going to use the same designer for your invitations to keep the style similar and consistent, so that's one fewer thing you need to worry about!

While Save the Dates should be sent at least a year before the date of the wedding, you won't need to order your invitations until four or five months before your date. Then, you can send the formal invitations out six weeks to three months to the day.

All the Info

Before you sign any contracts or place any orders, make sure you know what you're looking for. Know your colors, know your styles, and know whether you want to add any personal touches. You should also decide whether you want to include information such as the dress code (black tie? beach attire?), where you're registered (only on shower invites!), and your parents' names.

Parents' names are sometimes tricky, since first you have to figure out who is officially "hosting" the event, and then you have to figure out how they want to be listed on the invitation. Step parents, grandparents, foster parents, and any other type of caregiver who had a hand in raising you or supporting your relationship should be considered here.

Examples include:

MR. AND MRS. JOHN MARTIN AND MR. AND MRS. BOB BRENT
INVITE YOU TO SHARE IN THE WEDDING CELEBRATION OF
THEIR CHILDREN
ALEXANDRA MARTIN & TREVOR BRENT

MR. AND MRS. JOHN MARTIN
INVITE YOU TO SHARE IN THE WEDDING OF THEIR DAUGHTER
ALEXANDRA
TO
TREVOR BRENT
SON OF MR. AND MRS. BOB BRENT

And if neither party is claiming the role of "host" of your big event—or if you just want to keep the invitation simple and elegant—feel free to just include your own.

Once you know all these details (including who, what, when, where, and how to RSVP), you'll need to figure out what else you will need to send in the main envelope. Do you need a map for out-of-towners to use to get from the ceremony to the reception? Should the hotel at which your guests are staying be included on said map? Should you include an invitation for those who should attend the rehearsal dinner?

A quick search of any invitation designer's portfolio will show you all the different options involved in this part of the planning. Be inspired by what they've already put together and then create something of your own that represents the two of you.

Finding the Designer

Various options are available for your Save the Dates and invitations. For the DIY or hands-on couple, you can use a service such as VistaPrint or even Walmart's online photo department to print both. If an online site doesn't have the design you want for invitations, tweak other designs for postcards or greeting cards and make them into invites.

You can also hire a graphic designer or illustrator to create your invitations. This way, your invitations will match your theme, they will be personalized, and they will also be unique. However, you will pay more for this personal service.

Your photographer may also be able to get in on the invitation action, especially if you're planning to include a photo of you either on or in your invitation. Photographers are creative people; they may also moonlight as graphic designers or may employ them in their companies and will be able to make the invitations for you. If this is the case, try to get the invitations bundled with your wedding day or engagement photos and see if they'll cut you a break.

Tip!

Is your budget about to blow? Save some money here and send electronic invites. Create a wedding website, set up a Facebook group, or create a Google event and keep people informed. For those older or non-tech savvy guests, print a few e-invites and send them the hardcopies.

This is far from ideal for many traditional brides and grooms, but it's a very easy option if you need to save money and have the know-how to move the entire task online.

When you're purchasing your invitations, search for answers to the following questions if you're ordering from a website, or ask your designer:

- What's included in the price?
  - Save the Dates
  - Envelopes (outer, inner, and RSVP)
  - Labels
  - RSVP cards
  - Reception cards (separate from the ceremony invitation, unless they're in the same place or there will not be a ceremony)

- Accents: embossing, engraving, offsetting, calligraphy
- Thank-you notes and envelopes
- Favor tags
- Place cards
- Can you see a printed, hardcopy example before you commit to a large order?
- When will the entire batch be ready?
- What is the policy if they make a mistake? Will they cover the reprinting fee?
- Will they print extra to send to you in case of last-minute or lost invitations?
- Do they offer envelope-stuffing, stamping, and shipping?

If your invitation designer or packager will not stuff and ship the invitations for you (either at all or at a reasonable fee), it's time to enlist the help of your bridal party! Make it a fun night—keep the wine coming, the music loud, and the laughter going as long as you can. Take tons of breaks, eat something sweet, and keep all the booze and food away from the invites at all times!

Wedding Programs

Every wedding does not need a program, especially those that don't require a long (or any) ceremony. However, if you'd like to get them printed for yours, you'll need to decide who will design and print them, what will be in them, and who will pass them out.

Your invitation designer may be able to print the programs for you, matching your invitations and your overall style or theme. You may also decide to DIY this part of your wedding, saving some money and putting your own personal touches in them.

If your ceremony is on the longer side, you may want to include a breakdown of the day. If it will feature many readings and songs, you can include the names of the people reading or singing and the lyrics to the songs so everyone can participate. If you're including an ancient tradition in your ceremony, you may want to define the tradition (its history, its meaning, etc.) in your program.

If you did not include directions or a map to the reception space, you can add that to the programs, as well.

You may also want to list and thank the bridesmaids and groomsmen somewhere inside, especially if you enlist their help in handing out the programs to your attendees.

Make the programs your own, especially if you're designing them yourselves!

Stay Organized and Keep Track

When you know your final guest list, consider creating a spreadsheet with everyone's contact information so you can hand everything over to your invitation designers. Then, keep the spreadsheet and add a column for RSVP and guests.

As your start to hear from your guests, record that they have responded and also how many people they are bringing. If they're coming to the rehearsal dinner, make a mark in that column. If they're attending a post-wedding brunch, check it off. If they say no, mark it! If they want the chicken, the beef, the fish, or the vegetarian option, make sure you record that, too.

You don't need to do this as you receive every single RSVP. Instead, start a pile on Monday and enter all the RSVPs you receive for the week on Saturday night. If you're good with spreadsheets, use the codes to total the amount of people saying YES and NO, that way you know how many more you're waiting for as the date grows near.

Registering for Gifts

Like wedding band shopping, this is an area you and your fiancé can tackle on your own. If he or she (or you!) isn't really into the idea of registering and shopping isn't quite his or her thing, then you can take your mother or your father or your maid of honor along with you. Hand them a gun and get to work!

Some newlyweds move into their first homes together right after they're married. Others are already living together, but may

be planning to move to a bigger home or apartment. And then there are those couples who got their first mortgage before buying a ring or two and may already have everything they need.

If you don't want to register, you don't have to register. If you want to ask for cash or checks, you can do so—respectfully. If you want to set up a donation for your honeymoon or your future first home or your future children's college funds, you can do that, too.

But for those of us who have been looking forward to registering and need to figure out how to do so, the best place to start is to evaluate what you have and figure out exactly what you need. The most popular categories are china/flatware, kitchenware/kitchen appliances, bathroom/bedroom linens, and electronics. Though these are the traditional categories, you could really register for anything you think you'll need. If you recently purchased a home with a great backyard that you plan on entertaining in, maybe you need a new grill or patio furniture. Maybe you're really into game nights and need to build up your collection. Maybe you're an active couple and are really looking for hiking or snorkel gear. Or maybe you're not the entertainment type and instead you're working on building up empty rooms in the house, such as a library, home office, gym, or game room.

Once you know for what you'd like to register, then you can approach the stores in which you'd like to create registries. You can make an appointment at some, while others simply allow you to walk up to the Registry Desk during its specified hours. Depending on the store, you can even create your registry online.

While you're registering, make sure you keep the prices varied. Don't load the lists up with one expensive item after another; this will make it difficult for people to shop for you. In addition, don't be afraid to over-register. It's better to have more on your list than less; this will ensure everyone invited will find something to buy for you.

Registry Wows (and Whoas!)

"I registered at Belk and Bed, Bath & Beyond. The only things I got from my registry were towels. Lots and lots of towels. I also got about fifteen picture frames. But I did get this really cool hand painted chip and dip set from Mexico." —ARDI A.

"We registered for everything household-related. Got a TON of kitchen stuff. Second most was bathroom stuff, and some wall art and cute decorative things like that. Strangest gift? A—ahem—Kama sutra kit from our friend's mom. We did NOT register for that." —BRIANNA S.

"I registered at Crate and Barrel and Dillards, I think, for china. Registering for china and crystal was a huge mistake. I didn't grow up in a household that had or used china so it never occurs to me to use mine. Honestly, I'm more likely to use Chinet and red solo cups when having a big family celebration so I don't have to do dishes." —MELISSA L.

> "We wanted such an eclectic assortment of things that we didn't register anywhere; we made a list, gave it to my mom, and told people to get in touch with her about what we'd like." —SARAH C.

Seating Charts

You can work on your seating charts as you work on your tentative guest list, your final guest list, and your list of RSVP yes's. No matter what, be sure you have your final seating chart ready a full two weeks before the wedding. This will give your venue enough time to set up the room the way you want it.

You can put together your seating chart on the computer, or you can use a giant poster board with post-it notes—whichever fits your style best.

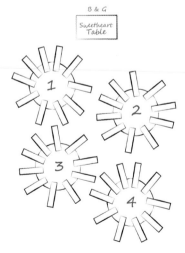

Although it may become a bit complicated, you're going to want to enlist the help of your bridesmaids, parents, future in-laws, and especially your spouse with this project. In an ideal world (or, if you've held your ground on your guest list!), you'll know every single person who attends your wedding. You'll know who everyone gets along with, what their personalities are like, and whether they can deal with a table of kids seated to their right. You'll also know whether they'll spend most of their night on the dance floor or up against the wall in a faraway corner.

However, you most likely won't know—or at least, know well—every single person attending your wedding. You may have never met some of your future spouse's cousins, you may not have seen Aunt Ida in twenty years, or you may not know anything about your mother's friend from work. This is where the others come in—those who *do* know these people.

Aside from the obvious approach—seating people together who will get along—you may also want to place them in the following groups:

- Your immediate family
- Your partner's immediate family
- Your extended family
- Your partner's extended family
- Your friends from high school/college/home
- Your partner's friends from high school/college/home
- Mutual friends of you both
- Your friends from work
- Your partner's friends from work
- Mixed table(s)
- The kids (if attending)

Where should the wedding party sit?

In addition to figuring out who will stand where and who will walk up and down the aisle with whom, you're going to have to figure out where your bridesmaids and groomsmen will sit. You have a couple of options here:

- Everyone at the front of the room, one big table, with you and your spouse in the middle
  - Bridesmaids on the bride's side, groomsmen on the groom's
  - Mixed parties; bridesmaid, groomsmen, bridesmaid, groomsmen
- You and your spouse at a sweetheart table up front, with your wedding party close by
- You and your spouse at a sweetheart table up front, with your wedding party scattered throughout various tables

Think about your wedding party. Where will each person be most comfortable? If their significant other isn't in the wedding, then that means that person will be seated alone, possibly at the Mixed Table, while their date is up in the front of the room. If anyone in your party is uncomfortable with all-eyes-on-them, then they've probably already had their fill of attention from the ceremony and introductions in the beginning of the reception, so they may not want to be at the front of the room at the big table.

If you can't decide what to do, feel free to ask your wedding party what they'd prefer. Majority wins.

Favors for Them

No matter your budget or how well you know everyone you invited, you should absolutely give them a gift or a favor to take home with them at the end of the night. These don't have to be expensive items, nor should they be different items per person. This is not the time to play favorites, to impress your boss, or to win your grandmother's affection. Every single guest should get the same exact gift, period.

These gifts don't have to be extravagant or expensive. They don't need to be heavily personalized, either. If you're going the personalized route, all you need to add are your names and the date of your wedding. You don't need to write a unique message on each label; your guests will know you appreciated their presence (and their presents!) when you send the thank-you notes later.

Your favors can be practical, such as magnets, bookmarks, small photo albums, or votive candle holders. They can be champagne flutes, coasters, matchbooks, or key chains. Or even tote bags, bottle openers, flash drives, or shot glasses. If

your wedding takes place during the holiday season, you can give everyone an ornament.

Favors can also be edible! Personalized M&M's and chocolate bars are cute, as are small dessert bags, miniature bottles of champagne or wine with your photo on the label, or little kits like "make your own lip balm" or "s'mores in a bag."

And then, there are the thoughtful favors. Instead of giving a gift, give a donation in your guests' names. As they leave, give them a small placard with information about the donation you've made.

Tip!

Don't drive yourself mad trying to find the most unique or most adorable favor your guests will ever see. You've already given your guests the gift of a great time and an opportunity to make memories with the people they love and even perhaps the chance to make new friends.

Gift Baskets

If you have a lot of guests coming in from out of town, and you have a bit of room in your budget, one of the sweeter things you can do to make their traveling easier is to have a small gift basket placed in their hotel room (or the room in which they're staying, even if it is your old bedroom at your parents' house).

These bags can be simple, but thoughtful. Consider placing necessities like water bottles, sodas, and little snacks inside; after all, some of your guests are probably tired from traveling and may have just consumed a nearly inedible in-flight meal. Plus, this will save them from the outrageous prices in their room's fridge or mini-bar.

If you have some more room in your budget, you can also include relaxing scents via shampoos, lotions, or bubble baths.

Candles are also an option, but check with the hotel first (and if it's okay, include a pack of matches).

Gifts for the Major Players

To show thanks to everyone involved in helping you plan your wedding, you should consider purchasing gifts separate from the favors all of the guests receive. Again, these gifts don't need to be budget-busters, but you should keep in mind that these people know what you spent on each invitation, each table setting, and each chair cover. If you give them something on the cheap side, they may feel that you didn't truly appreciate all their help.

Bridesmaids, bridesmen, groomsmen, and groomsgals

Traditionally, these men and women receive some type of jewelry and accessory that they can wear to your wedding. They all receive identical gifts that go with their wedding attire (perhaps cuff links, necklaces, or bracelets) that they can also wear to formal occasions or every day, depending on the style of the gift.

If you're looking to provide something a bit more comfortable, you can give the ladies monogramed yoga pants or can get tasteful hoodies or T-shirts made for the entire party.

You also don't need to go the to-be-worn route with your gifts to your wedding party. You can buy them a stack of movie tickets, admission to their favorite theme park, gift cards to the best local restaurants, or something they can hang or use in their homes.

Your bridesmaid and best man should receive a little something extra if they've put in the extra work typically demanded of these positions. You can either buy them additional gifts, or you can make their gifts (still similar to the others') stand out in some way—either by color or quality.

You should give them their gifts a week or two before your wedding, especially if you want them to wear whatever you bought them on or before the wedding day.

Note: If you're chipping in on their bridesmaids dresses, tuxes, hair, or makeup for the day, take this into account when you're deciding how much to spend on these gifts.

Flower girls or ring bearers
Depending on the age of the children in your wedding, you may be able to impress them with stuffed animals, comic books, chapter or picture books, video games, dolls, fun kits (science, makeup, dress-up), or gift cards to their favorite places.

This doesn't have to be hard; they're going to love simply receiving something they can unwrap and show off. Ask their parents if you can't think of something age-appropriate or you don't know their interests.

Parents
If your parents are especially involved or helpful in the wedding planning process, you should thank them in some way. Your gift should more personal than those you give to a host or a vendor. You should put some thought into it and really make sure you're giving them something either practical or sentimental.

Think about what they need and try to fill that void. You could also purchase them something thoughtful, such as a weekend at a spa or offer to pay the bill at the restaurant of their choice. You can buy your father football tickets or your mother a two-hour deep-tissue massage.

Or you can present them with your favorite photo of the four of you together, be it on your wedding day or beforehand. If this is the avenue you want to take, then try to plan a few occasions before your wedding so you can get the photo you're after. Holidays and family gatherings are a great start.

Hosts, wedding planner, or devoted vendor
If anyone has opened up their home for your use in any way (hosting guests, preparation the day-of, baking desserts, etc.), you should also call attention to how grateful you are for them. You can send them flowers, you can sign them up for a wine-of-the-month club, or you can give them something for their home, like a new quilt, vase, or picture frame—something to show that you appreciate them opening up their home for you on your special day.

You're already paying your wedding planner for his or her services, so you don't need to get too caught up in your thank-you gift to them. A gift card to a restaurant or store they mentioned could be enough, as long as you stick it in the appropriate card.

Same goes for your vendors. If any go above and beyond expectations, feel free to drop them a note, give them an extra tip, or make them a dessert bag. If you really enjoyed working with them, send them a small thank-you basket when everything is over, cleaned up, and paid for.

Writing Your Vows and/or Your Ceremony

Many brides and grooms fear the day they have to write their vows. They get all worked up over finding the perfect words that will be sure to impress—but who are they trying to impress?

The only person you need to write to and for is your future spouse. Don't worry about what your mom or your sister or your high school English teacher will say about your vows. It's all about your partner—the man or woman standing directly across from you.

Don't overthink this process. Simply grab a pen and some paper or sit down at your computer and write what your future spouse means to you. You don't need to recall specific memories, you don't need to include inside jokes. The words you say don't need to be linked to your wedding's theme. All you need to do is tell your partner you love them and you never want to be without them. That's it!

Keep It Simple!

Too many of us fret over the words we'll say to our partners on our wedding day. Do yourself a favor and don't include any words in your vows that you either don't know the meaning of or can't pronounce! It doesn't matter how smart or romantic you may sound if you get it right. Instead, you'll spend all day worrying about pronouncing it incorrectly and you may accidently flub it based on those nerves alone. Keep your vocabulary—and your message—simple.

I love you. You love me. Let's do this!

Your vows don't need to be pages and pages long, either. If you're memorizing them, you certainly don't want them to be lengthy. And if your ceremony is one of the longer ones, you don't want to be on your feet any longer than you already have been. Keep them simple and keep them short; if you want to write a love letter to your future bride or groom, do it—and give it to them later!

Although you can technically work on your wedding vows right up to the last minute (and many of us do—that's nothing to be ashamed of!), you don't want to wait that long to nail down the details of your ceremony. You are the only one who will recite your vows, so if you wait to write them, you're the only person affected by your procrastination. However, if you're writing your own ceremony, you're going to want to finish it and distribute it to all involved no later than three months before your wedding day.

If you're getting married at a specific location that has, say, a priest who will recite the ceremony, you may not need to plan your ceremony—or you may only contribute a bit to the entire program because certain things need to happen no matter what (such as communion or the singing of specific psalms).

If you're bringing in your own officiant or you're able to design your own ceremony then consider the following outline, adapted from the American Marriage Ministries' format. Included here are descriptions of each step and some questions you should consider as you plan.

Note

This is the traditional ceremony outline, but feel free to put your own twist on it. Plan to include songs, poems, readings, or other performance pieces between these main parts. Just make sure that the program you develop flows smoothly and is not clunky or disorganized. The average ceremony is fifteen to twenty minutes long, so try to keep that mind, as well—especially if your guests are all standing around you and not seated comfortably.

Processional
The entrance of those involved in the ceremony.

- Will music play? Will someone sing?
- Who will walk? Bridal party? Groomsmen? Flower girl?
- Do you have any remote members of the wedding party who need to be Skyped in?
- Who will accompany you down the aisle? And your spouse?

Invocation
The welcoming of your guests and a description of what they are gathered to witness.

- How will the officiant greet your guests?
- What do you want him/her to say about the two of you, as individuals and as a couple?

Exchange of Vows
Take the time to tell each other how you feel now and will forever feel while at each other's sides.

- Will you say your own vows?
- Will you repeat the vows recited by the officiant?

Declaration of Intent

Confirmation of your commitment to one another. The AMM says this is like the verbal signing of a marriage license.

- How should your officiant phase this question?
- Which response will you give? (I do. I will. Etc.)
- Should your officiant ask if anyone present objects to their union?

Ring Exchange

The physical exchanging of your vows, via the rings. This is one part of the ceremony that many choose not to customize, as the officiant typically asks the couple to repeat the words, "With this ring, I thee wed."

- Will you incorporate a specific tradition or ritual into this exchange? Examples include lighting a candle, tying a knot, saying a prayer, or taking a moment of silence.
- Who will give you the rings? Ring bearer? Best man?

Pronouncement

The official announcement and the first kiss of your married life together!

- How should the officiant announce you? This typically begins with, "By the power vested in me by the State of . . ."
- What kind of kiss should you exchange?

Recessional

The officiant introduces you to your guests and then it's time to party!

- How do you want your officiant to announce you? (Mr. and Mrs. Smith? Mrs. and Mrs. Black? Mr. White and Mrs. Smith?)

- Who walks out when?
- Who is part of the receiving line?
- Will anything be thrown? Rice, flowers? Bubbles?
- Where are you going when you get to the end of the aisle?

Vow Renewals or Encore Weddings

Approximately one-fourth of today's weddings are what we call encore weddings, or ceremonies held to celebrate a couple who has previously been wed and want to renew their vows.

Just because it's your second time down the aisle doesn't mean it should be any less special; there's no reason you can't do the whole ceremony—or even go longer than you did the first time. Chances are, there are more people in your life now who you want to be part of your day. If you've had children, perhaps you want them to walk down the aisle, recite a vow for the family, or receive something in the jewelry exchange.

Celebrate this day!

Hair and Makeup

As with dress shopping and cake tasting, you're going to want to try out the best hair and makeup styles before you commit to one for your big day. Flip through magazines and pick a few looks to test. If you have a specific stylist in mind who will be with you on your wedding day, schedule a few appointments with him or her in the salon about one or two months beforehand

to try various styles. Bring photos of your dress and color scheme so they can make appropriate decisions and contributions to the look you're going for.

Note: Book your stylist, makeup artist, and nail artist (if you're having them done the day of) at least three months before your wedding, especially if you're getting married during peak wedding season. Many can do two weddings in a day, but you need to allow them for time to travel and catch their breath.

If one of your bridesmaids will be doing your hair and makeup, perhaps try a few looks out during a meeting of the bridal party. Drink some wine, try some hair styles, apply makeup, and compare. Discuss how you want your bridal party to wear their hair (if you even care—some of us don't) and ask them if your fake eyelashes are a bit too . . . fake.

Or maybe you're really skilled with a brush and a blow dryer and you're going to do your own getup. This is fine, too, and may save you a bunch of money. If this is what's going to make you most comfortable, don't allow anyone to pressure you into hiring a professional.

Be sure to also stand your ground when someone is hovering over you with bright blue eye shadow in one hand and a hair straightener in the other. If you don't want to wear dark red lipstick, then don't let them apply it. If you're really not worried about one stray curl, then don't let them touch it—especially in the moments right before the ceremony starts. The closer it is to go-time, the more frantic people feel, and the better the chances they'll make a mistake than fix something that wouldn't have bothered you in the first place.

Honeymoon Details

According to The Knot, the word *honeymoon* originated with the Ancient Teuton weddings, which were always held under a full moon and followed by the consumption of honey wine during the thirty days following their ceremony. Although many couples sip a lot of wine on their honeymoons, most of these celebratory travels don't last a month, nor do they take place immediately after the wedding.

It's becoming more common to put honeymoons on hold, either due to budget restraints or simply being unable to take time away from work or school. Some couples travel for their one-year anniversary, some wait until their fifth. Some go away for a long weekend somewhere close to home, while others may simply stay at a bed and breakfast for an extra day and then return to the grind. Don't feel pressured to take your honeymoon if you can't fit it into your life right now. If there are more important things, put it off and make it more special later.

If you are honeymooning directly after your wedding day, though, you're going to want to make sure you have everything planned and purchased months beforehand. Approach these plans like you would any other travel plans—stick to your budget, know where you want to go, figure out what you're going to want to do when you get there, and make sure you're packed for appropriate weather and terrain. Along the way, don't be afraid to mention to the travel agent, hotel concierge, or anyone else with whom you interact that you'll be on your honeymoon—perhaps you'll get a few perks!

According to the Travel Channel, the five most popular wedding destinations in recent years have been:

- Camino Real Acapulco Diamante, Mexico
- The Bellagio Hotel, Las Vegas, Nevada, United States
- Fairmont Chateau Lake Louise, Canada
- Walt Disney World, Florida, United States
- Amankila, Indonesia

You can go anywhere and do anything for your honeymoon; the trip should represent what the two of you love most. If you like to immerse yourself in foreign cultures, do it. If you like to stay close to home, do it. If you don't drink, go to a dry beach. If you hate flying, try a train or a road trip! Go for a hike, lie in the sand, pitch a tent, or spend a few nights in a cabin near a waterfall in the woods. The location itself doesn't need to be romantic; bring the romance with you, if that's what you want!

Where'd you go for your honeymoon?

"I went to Sandals in St. Lucia! The best part was that it was all inclusive, so we didn't have to worry about anything while we were there." —ARDI A.

"We haven't gone on our honeymoon yet, but when we do, we're going to Greece!" —GWEN C.

"Vegas, baby!! We love being out west. We stayed for a week; there's so much to do there!" —JOCELYN G.

"We did a big Disney trip! Four-day Disney cruise and then stayed at Disney for the rest of the trip. The cruise was a first for us and we stayed at one of the higher-end resorts in Disney and were upgraded and pampered because we were in our honeymoon. Loved every minute." —CHRISTINA M.

"We went to a Sandals resort, too! Whitehouse, Jamaica. We loved it because it was all-inclusive. We were super lazy though—never even left the resort. We just drank and ate and slept!" —JESS L.

"We took a cruise from Spain to France and Italy. We really wanted to go to Europe and thought it was the perfect time to go! We were there for about a week and a half. We really enjoyed that we were at a different port every day! Not sure if I would do another cruise again, but definitely a great trip!" —KATE R.

"Jamaica! Four days. The entire trip was amazing . . . except for the deep sea fishing. We paid a lot of money to have an entire day ruined." —KHAYLA F.

"Disney World! A week, because that was where he proposed! Best part was going to the exact same luau we did when he proposed." —BRIANNA S.

Your After To-Do List

Wedding festivities don't end when the dress comes off. In fact, you're going to have a ton of things to do in the days and weeks following the celebration. These may start off with a brunch the morning after the reception, returning any rented equipment, travel for the honeymoon, and a flurry of social media inquiries from people who either didn't know you were even dating each other or who want to know all about the wedding because they couldn't make it.

In addition to all that, you're also going to have to remember to do the following:

- Exchange/return gifts you don't need/won't use
- Return any rented gowns or tuxes/suits
- Complete your contracts with your vendors; be sure all bills are paid and vendors are tipped
- Donate leftover gift baskets/favors
- Write and send thank-you notes
- Get your marriage license (unless you did this pre-ceremony)
- File all paperwork if you're going to change your name (and visit your bank)
- Print and frame wedding photos; distribute as necessary

10

Your Wedding Day

"Go confidently into the direction of your dreams! Live the life
you've imagined."
—THOREAU

• • •

As your wedding day approaches, you're going to experience
a slew of different emotions, but try to keep your head on
straight and put your wedding party to work! You're going to
have to tie up some loose ends, pack a few bags (and even more
if you're heading straight out for your honeymoon!), and run a
few errands, but it'll all be worth it in a few days!

One Week Before

If you haven't finalized your vows, seating chart, or notes on
décor for the reception and ceremony spaces yet, this is the time
to do it. If your wedding is more formal than most, you may

also want to check in with anyone you think may be planning on toasting you and your partner during the reception. If you have a specific plan or schedule you're following, you'll need to know when they're giving their toast to make sure everything will stay on time.

This is also a really good time to work out a schedule or check-list for your wedding day if you haven't done so already. Depending on the style of the two of you as a couple, you may have decided to fly by the seat of your pants and just let everything happen as it's supposed to—or you may have been planning everything down to the minute from the entrance to the cake cutting to the last dance. If you want to make a loose schedule to share with your wedding party, just so they know where they have to be and when, finalize that this week, too.

After you deliver these pieces to whoever needs them, it's time to make sure you have all the data you need. Make an Excel sheet or a running list of contact information for all of your vendors and then make copies for everyone in the wedding party. On your day, you're not going to want to worry about whether the DJ showed up or whether a limo got lost. To ensure your wedding party knows who to contact, be sure to give them a hardcopy as well as a digital file (send it to their emails so they can refer to it on their phones).

Once this is out of the way, confirm all of the appointments you have for the day before or the day of the wedding. This may include manicures and pedicures, hair appointments, or even massages or spa-type activities. If your maid of honor wants to make these calls and get confirmation, let her!

This week is also the week for running last-minute errands. You should go to the bank and retrieve enough cash to tip your vendors at the end of the night. Organize the tips in clearly labeled envelopes and make sure they're in your bag and ready to go. You probably won't know the names of any most of the people who will be helping out that day, but if you put the business name or supervisor name on the envelope, it should find its way to the right person.

Make this the week you pick up your marriage license, too. Do some online searching (or ask someone who has gotten married in your area) and find out where you need to go, what you need to bring with you, and if you can just walk in or if you need to make an appointment. (In most states, you and your partner are going to have to go to the office together, so make sure this fits into both of your schedules.) You'll most likely be directed to City Hall, and you're probably going to need photo IDs, birth certificates, and proof of residence. Some states also require blood tests. If you or your spouse has previously

been married, you may also need to provide proof of your divorce or your previous partner's passing.

The reason you should wait until the week before (or at least around that time) is because, depending on the state, the license may only be good for a few days or weeks. If you aren't legally married before the

It's Getting Hot in Here

If your wedding is indoors, you may want to call the reception hall/venue a few days before the wedding to ask if they will be able to set the temperature at a specific degree. If it's winter, ask them to make sure the heat isn't blasting and, if it's summer, ask them how cool the main room will be throughout the night. You don't want your guests to be uncomfortable.

license expires, you'll have to apply for another. Once you're officially married, have your officiant sign the license and then mail it to or drop it off at City Hall.

Finally, sometime before the rehearsal dinner, plan a lunch, dinner, or happy hour with your entire wedding party to thank them for all the help they've provided over the past few weeks, months, or years. If you haven't done so already, this is a great time to give them your gifts.

One Day Before

This would be a fantastic day for that aforementioned massage!

Although you should be doing your best to relax and just enjoy the excitement, you should also be paying attention the weather today. If it looks like it may rain and you're planning on an outdoor wedding, call your wedding party to attention and make sure your Plan B is in order. Do you have the tents? Is the reception area ready to set up the backup ceremony space? If it's going to be sweltering, call the venue and ask them if they have fans they could use to create a gentle breeze. Don't let Mother Nature catch you by surprise!

On this day, you should also run down your wedding day checklist to make sure you have everything you'll need. You may also want to pack an emergency kit that may contain items such as extra panty hose, double-sided tape, safety pins, stain removers, tissues, cell phone charger, hairspray, dental floss, tweezers, and Band-Aids. Every bride's kit will be different from the next, and a quick Internet search will help you figure out what all to put in there.

While you're tying up the last of the loose ends, it's important to take time out to simply enjoy your company. Let everyone else put out the fires (good practice for tomorrow!) and spend a few hours with your out-of-state cousins and your great-grandmother. Spend some quality time with your new sister-in-law while you get ready for the wedding rehearsal and the following dinner.

Play it safe!

Don't try anything new on this day! Don't put on new perfumes, lotions, or makeup. Don't pluck your eyebrows in a different shape than you're used to. Don't try a new yoga pose or go for a run if you're not a runner. Don't eat or drink anything you've never consumed before. If you have a bad reaction to any of this, you may be sore, miserable, or very sick for your ceremony tomorrow. Skip the potential allergic reactions and food poisonings and stick to what you know today.

Finally, at the rehearsal dinner, just have a good time! If there's music, dance! If there's cake, eat! If there's wine, drink! (But not too much—who wants to be nauseous or hungover walking down the aisle?) Thank your family and friends for being there and enjoy their company.

The Night Before

Although tradition used to dictate that the bride and the groom should sleep alone the night before their wedding, and then not see each other until the ceremony the day of, fewer couples are honoring this one these days. It's no coincidence, considering more than 50 percent of couples live together before marriage. If you're getting married in the town in which you live, you may as well sleep in your own bed and start your wedding day together.

If it's important to you to keep this tradition, or if your religion or faith requires this of you both, then say goodnight after the rehearsal dinner! You can talk on the phone and text or pass notes between your assigned areas at the venue if you need to—just make sure that if you make this decision, you commit to it.

The Day Of: Maid of Honor and Best Man Responsibilities

Everyone has to play their part to make sure your wedding goes off without a hitch. If you've prepared a schedule, be sure everyone in your wedding party, your parents, and your wedding planner has a copy. In addition, if you've printed programs to give your ceremony attendees and reception guests, they'll also know what will be happening and when. There are specific duties, however, that your maid/matron of honor and your best man should be performing on this day.

Maid of Honor

Aside from keeping everyone in the bridal party on schedule, the maid (or man) of honor is tasked with being the bride's right-hand gal (or guy) from dawn to dusk. She should keep an eye on the bride before the ceremony, making sure she doesn't eat or drink too much or too little. She should keep the mood light and make sure the bride is under as little stress as possible.

During the ceremony, the maid of honor should fix the bride's dress and veil/train when she takes her spot at the altar. She should also hold the bride's bouquet and provide the groom's ring when it comes time. After the ceremony, the maid of honor will sign the wedding certificate/license and then escort the bride to the photo shoot if one is scheduled.

At the reception, the maid of honor should also, once again, be sure the bride is eating. She should also give a toast and socialize with the guests. After the reception, she should help the bride take off her dress and make sure it's stored correctly.

Best Man

The best man (or woman) has similar responsibilities to the maid of honor. He needs to make sure everyone standing up for the groom is on time and following the schedule. He needs to keep the groom grounded, well-fed, and hydrated. He should hold the bride's wedding band during the reception and he should sign the wedding license after.

At the reception, he'll give a toast to the couple, he'll socialize with the guests, and he'll make sure the wedding party acts responsibility (while simultaneously having a great time!). At the end of the night, he should make sure all the guests have a sober ride home. He should call cabs or limos for anyone who can't drive themselves.

The Day Of: You and Your Spouse

This is it! Your wedding day is here. You're nervous, you're happy, you're excited, you're a little scared. There's so much to process, so much to remember, so much to experience. Have some coffee or tea in the morning, spend some time relaxing, and then dive right in!

Pre-Ceremony DO's and DON'T's

DO

- **. . . consider pre-wedding photos while you get ready.** Some of the most stunning photos are taken while the bride and groom are putting on their final accessories and anticipating the walk down the aisle.
- **. . . keep your head clear and calm.** Avoid stress and fighting whenever possible. Take deep breaths and keep your feet on the ground.
- **. . . hand over all control.** As you practiced yesterday, it's time to let your wedding planner, maid of honor, best

man, father, mother, sister, etc. take care of the details.
Let them do your dirty work. Have a glass of champagne
while they fight with the limo driver.

- **. . . allow yourself to have fun!** (Remember that glass
of champagne?) Enjoy the company and support you've
surrounded yourself with and stay loose while you're
getting ready.
- **. . . use the bathroom before you put your dress on,
ladies.** No further explanation needed.

DON'T

- **. . . allow yourself to become dehydrated.** Avoid drinking
too much champagne and not enough water.
- **. . . allow yourself to become overhydrated.** Avoid
drinking too much water, as the last thing on your mind
when you walk down the aisle should be how badly you
have to pee.
- **. . . eat too little.** If your stomach is entirely empty, you
may become dizzy or disorientated during the excitement
of the ceremony and reception.
- **. . . eat too much.** If your stomach is too full, you may
want to sleep instead of dance. You also risk feeling
nauseous as well as bloating if you eat the wrong type of
food.
- **. . . get drunk or high.** Stay in the moment and let the
anticipation and the excitement of what's coming move
you through it.
- **. . . smoke cigarettes.** Though the health risk should
probably always be a concern, this is more about smelling
fresh and clean for your partner and for everyone

who is going to congratulate you with hugs and kisses throughout the day. The scent of cigarettes clings to everything—wedding dresses, no matter the fabric, are not exempt.

- **. . . go overboard with the makeup.** This applies to both men and women, as some men may want to be powdered if they tend to be a little shiny under direct lights. A little goes a long way on this day. Don't use dark eye shadow and avoid the cake face!

- **. . . avoid anything new.** As previously discussed, don't try anything new today. Avoid fake eyelashes if you've never worn them, don't drink coconut water if you've never had it, and don't cover yourself in a friend's lotion if you've never used it before. A negative reaction can ruin your entire day.

- **. . . wear uncomfortable underwear no matter what.** If you're dying to dig your panties or your briefs out of your butt all night, you're going to be distracted and uncomfortable instead of elated and carefree.

At the Ceremony

You've already rehearsed this—hell, you may have even written every line the officiant is going to speak. The important thing to do is pay attention during the ceremony. Watch for the cues so you know when to walk, stand, sit, and kneel. Listen to the officiant, listen to the readings and the songs, and listen to your spouse when he or she speaks their vows. This is the first time you're hearing them, so block out everything else and take them in.

What shouldn't you do during your ceremony? You shouldn't worry about making mistakes! You shouldn't worry about flubbing your vows, tripping over your dress a little, or dropping the ring on the exchange. If any of this happens, laugh it off with your guests and keep going. They'll think it's adorable, and you'll have a fun story to tell later!

At the end of the ceremony, be sure to kiss your husband or wife! It doesn't have to be a deep, passionate kiss. It should be whatever you're both comfortable with. Throw in a hug or a secret handshake if you really want to. Just be sure to give the people what they want!

On the way out, you'll most likely form a receiving line to say receive congratulation from your ceremony attendees. In this line will be your parents, your spouse's parents, and possibly your grandparents and siblings. Every receiving line is different today, so don't feel like you *have* to follow any guidelines for this part.

What's your favorite memory from your wedding day?

"When my bridesmaids put on my dress. It had to go over my head and my hair was done, so they wrapped me in butcher paper and slid the dress over that. It was ridiculous and hilarious and I have a picture of it." —LISA R.

"Walking down the aisle with my father towards John. Everything became like a reality at that point and all eyes are on you from friends and family. Crying, but tears of joy! That's when it all felt real! And vows were also very special because it was an intimate moment between the two of us that we got to share with friends and family!" —LINDSAY S.

→→→→→ ←←←←←

"#1. After the ceremony and the reception, we finally had a chance to eat our cake once in our suite. They say you can't taste cold/frozen things, but we tasted the decadence of the day. #2 During the reception: we purposefully ran outside (into the cold November night) just to take a minute to look in at our friends and family celebrating love. The cold suddenly did not matter, as the candle lights from within, smiles, and warm embraces were all that we could see. #3 (best for last) The smile of my wife while walking down the aisle." —DAVE L.

→→→→→ ←←←←←

"My favorite memory was seeing Jeff for the first time walking down the aisle." —CHRISTINA M.

→→→→→ ←←←←←

"We got married outside. A friend played guitar to set the mood, and when we came out to take center stage together, no lie, a rooster wandering the grounds decided to crow, heralding the event. We were delighted and everyone still laughs about it to this day." —MARIA T.

At the Photo Shoot

Simply have a good time during this part! Be natural, and don't allow the photographer to bully you into any poses that may make you or anyone in your party feel uncomfortable. (If you're afraid your girls are going to fall out of your dress if you have to keep doing those jumping poses, then tell him it's not your thing and find another pose.) Make sure you get photos with everyone in the wedding party in all different types of combinations.

At the Reception

Traditionally, the bride and groom skip cocktail hour in exchange for time with the photographer and by themselves. However, if you want to go to your own cocktail hour, then go! This is your wedding; do what you want!

Once cocktail hour is over and everyone's settled in the reception area, you'll be introduced to your guests. Note that if you choose not to change your last name, you're going to want to let your emcee know ahead of time how he should introduce the two of you. In some cases, it may be easier to have him or her use your first names.

After you are introduced, you'll have your first dance. Let your wedding party know whether you want to dance the song together, uninterrupted, or if you expect other couples to eventually join you. This, again, is up to you. If you want the moment all to yourselves, take it. If you hate the spotlight, aren't a fan of dancing, and would feel more comfortable with a bustling dance floor surrounding you, feel free to call other couples onto the floor after the first minute or so.

Before dinner is served, start to work the room. Say hello to out-of-town guests, thank everyone for coming, take all the pictures you can. You need to be social today, even if it's not exactly something you love doing. Everyone is here for you and your partner; the least you could do is thank them for coming.

During dinner, be sure to eat! So many brides discover too late in the evening that they didn't eat enough or at all. You're paying for your food, so eat it! Having food in your stomach will also help you soak up all the alcohol. Although you'll most certainly enjoy the buzz, the last thing you'll want to do is black out on your wedding night.

At some point, toasts will be made in your honor. You and your partner should also consider giving one to thank everyone who helped you make the day possible—your parents; your wedding party; any friends or family members who baked, stuffed envelopes, or hosted guests in their home; your wedding planner; the venue, etc. It doesn't have to be a long toast, but they'll appreciate it all the same.

After dinner, you'll cut the cake. Again, it's up to you whether you want to feed each other like civilized human beings or shove the cake, fondant, and frosting into each other's faces. Discuss this beforehand; you really don't want to piss off your new husband or wife a few hours into being married. Don't forget to save the cake topper or the top tier! Tradition says you should freeze it and eat it on your one-year anniversary.

The rest of the night may be filled with customs based on your family, your faith, or your religion. You may participate in Saptapadi, the recitation of the hamotzie blessing, the combining of two glasses of wine from different vineyards, Tarantella folk dancing, or even sword dancing. You may also toss the bouquet and the garter if you so choose. But, again, your wedding, your choice.

The End of the Night

As the night comes to an end, if you notice the party is still active and exciting and everyone's still on the dance floor (and you have some room in your budget), ask the DJ if he can stay for another hour and ask the bar if they could stay open, too. Send your wedding planner to negotiate this if you've hired one. If you can, just keep going! This is your night!

When it's finally time to leave the venue, make an announcement and let your guests know where the after party is. Thank everyone as they come to say goodbye to you . . . and then continue the party at the next stop!

Have the time of your life with your friends and family, and then go home to continue the celebration with your new husband or wife.

Congratulations, and best wishes to you both!

Quotes

All you have to do is Google and you'll come up with an unimaginable amount of quotations on love, marriage, weddings, and relationships. These are just a small sampling of some of my favorites, found in various spots across the Internet. Feel free to use some of these quotations on your invitations/ save the dates, place cards, cake, etc.

"The highest happiness on earth is marriage."
—WILLIAM LYON PHELPS

"A successful marriage requires falling in love many times, always with the same person."
—MIGNON MCLAUGHLIN

"We don't take ourselves too seriously, and laughter is the best form of unity, I think, in a marriage."
—MICHELLE OBAMA

"Love is a symbol of eternity. It wipes out all sense of time, destroying all memory of a beginning and all fear of an end."
—UNKNOWN

"A married couple are well suited when both partners feel the need for a quarrel at the same time."
—JEAN ROSTAND

"Are we not like two volumes of one book?"
—MARCELINE DESBORDES-VALMORE

"What counts in making a happy marriage is not so much how compatible you are, but how you deal with incompatibility."
—LEO TOLSTOY

"Love is a game that two can play and both win."
—EVA GABOR

"Trip over love, you can get up. Fall in love and you fall forever."
—UNKNOWN

"For marriage to be a success, every woman and every man should have her and his own bathroom. The end."
—CATHERINE ZETA-JONES

"A good marriage is like a good trade: each thinks he got the better deal."
—IVERN BALL

"Love is everything it's cracked up to be… It really is worth fighting for, being brave for, risking everything for."
—ERICA JONG

"Being deeply loved by someone gives you strength; loving someone deeply gives you courage."
—LAO TZU

"Those who love deeply never grow old; they may die of old age, but they die young."
—DOROTHY CANFIELD FISHER

"There are all kinds of love in this world but never the same love twice."
—F. SCOTT FITZGERALD

"What a happy and holy fashion it is that those who love one another should rest on the same pillow."
—NATHANIEL HAWTHORNE

"Motto for the bride and groom: We are a work in progress with a lifetime contract."
—PHYLLIS KOSS

"Success in marriage does not come merely through finding the right mate, but through being the right mate."
—BARNETT R. BRICKNER

"Affection is responsible for nine-tenths of whatever solid and durable happiness there is in our lives."
—C. S. LEWIS

"When you realize you want to spend the rest of your life with somebody, you want the rest of your life to start as soon as possible."
—NORA EPHRON, *When Harry Met Sally*

"Time is too slow for those who wait, too swift for those who fear, too long for those who grieve, too short for those who rejoice, but for those who love, time is eternity."
—HENRY VAN DYKE

"Grow old with me! The best is yet to be!"
—ROBERT BROWNING

"For you see, each day I love you more / Today more than yesterday and less than tomorrow."
—ROSEMONDE GERARD

A Few Links for You

If you're interested in renting your wedding dress, bridesmaids dresses, or tuxes/suits, browse the following websites to see if you spot something that will fit your special day:

- Borrowing Magnolia | https://www.borrowingmagnolia.com/
- Rent the Runway | https://www.renttherunway.com
- Union Station | http://www.unionstation.com/
- Vow to Be Chic | http://www.vowtobechic.com/
- Weddington Way | https://www.weddingtonway.com/

If you do most of your research on your phone or tablet, or you want to find a way to get your friends and family involved even if they don't live nearby, try these following apps:

- Appy Couple | https://itunes.apple.com/us/app/appy-couple/id492345619?mt=8
- WedPics | https://www.wedpics.com/
- WedSocial | http://wedsocial.com/
- Wedding Wire | http://www.weddingwire.com/wedding-apps
- Wedding Party | https://www.weddingpartyapp.com/

Resources

Websites

"Average Wedding Cost." CostofWedding.com <http://www.costofwedding.com/>

Dawn, Randee. "Are diamonds really a girl's best friend? What your ring may say about your marriage." Today.com. October 8, 2014. <http://www.today.com/style/what-cost-your-engagement-ring-may-say-about-your-marriage-2D80202658?cid=sm_t_main_1_20141008_33124966>

Gringberg, Emanuella. "Report: More women moving in before marriage." CNN.com. April 4, 2013. <http://www.cnn.com/2013/04/04/living/women-premarital-cohabitation/>

Guth, Tracy. "Picking the Perfect Wedding Date." WeddingClub.com.au. <http://theknot.ninemsn.com.au/engagement/just-engaged/what-to-do-first/picking-the-perfect-wedding-date>

Heing, Bridey. "And this is the most bridesmaids anybody's ever had at a wedding." HelloGiggles.com. April 23, 2015.

<http://hellogiggles.com/bridesmaids-anybodys-ever-wedding/>

"Marriage Quotes That Will Help You Cope with Wedding Stress." HuffingtonPost.com. May 9, 2013. <http://www.huffingtonpost.com/2013/05/09/marriage-quotes_n_3241331.html>

Schneider, Meg. "Understanding How Dates and Times Affect Wedding Costs." Dummies.com. <http://www.dummies.com/how-to/content/understanding-how-dates-and-times-affect-wedding-c.html>

Tamaki, Stacie. "Veil FAQ's from the website of The Flirty Bride." TheFlirtyGuide.com <http://theflirtyguide.com/pages_FAQ/FAQ_how_to_choose_a_bridal_veil.html>

Books

Bare, Kelly. *The DIY Wedding*. Chronicle Books: San Francisco, CA, 2007.

Denny, Carrie and Paul Kepple. *The Bride's Instruction Manual*. Quirk Books: Philadelphia, PA, 2009.

Naylor, Sharon. *The Bride's Survival Guide*. Adams Media: Avon, MA, 2009.

O'Connell, Mark. *Modern Brides and Modern Grooms*. Skyhorse Publishing: New York, 2014.

Roney, Carly. *The Knot Book of Wedding Lists*. Clarkson Potter: New York, 2007.

Weiss, Mandy and Lisbeth Levine. *The Wedding Book*. Workman Publishing Company: New York, 2007.

Acknowledgments

As Gloria Steinmen said, "Being married is like having somebody permanently in your corner; it feels limitless, not limited." So, thank you to my future husband, Matthew, who could not be more supportive, open-minded, and level-headed while we plan our own nuptials. I love that you want to be as involved as you do because, after writing this book, I'm kind of wedding-ed out!

I'd also like to thank my mother, Bernadette Frail, and my sister and maid of honor, Kerri Frail, who tried their hardest to be patient while I insisted on finishing this project before starting my own wedding planning. I promise, I will now look at all the dresses you've pinned, venues you've listed, and wedding favors you've texted me about. And another thank-you to Kerri for illustrating this beautiful book. You're one of my favorite people to work with!

Shout outs to my father, Jeff Frail; my brother and groomsmen, Jeffrey; my own bridesmaids, Constance Renfrow, Kristen Magda, and Cathryn Frear Butler, and my bridesman, Andrew Seaman, for their advice, ideas, and encouragement during this project despite the physical distance between us.

And finally, thank you to everyone who contributed quotes from my "real-life" brides and grooms about their experiences wedding planning. I appreciate the conversations we've had and your willingness to share these moments with me. Thank you to: Ardi Alspach, Jessica Leake, Lindsay Smith, Melissa Lendhardt, Gwen Cole, Brianna Shrum, Khayla Griffiths, Marie Jaskulka, Kate Reilly, Natasha Sinel, Stace Keiser, Crystal Snarski, Jen Buckwash, Sarah Chrisman, Julie Ganz, Christina Magda, Lynn Mounce, Gabriel Squailia, Tom Reilly, Dave Lewis, Jocelyn Gebhardt, Jolene Guignet, Angela Harmon, and Lisa Reynolds. Also, thank you to my aunts, Filomena Nelson, Marie Warren, and Gloria Boots, for the support and the stories!

A big thank-you to Katherine Cassell, who provided me background information from the point-of-view of a wedding planner. You were great to work with! You, too, Sara Brosious! I appreciate everything you taught me about the accessories, a very vital part to any wedding! And to Lei Shishak, whose Q&A was definitely the last-minute frosting on the cake!

Index

Accessories, for dress shopping, 95
Acts (entertainment), 65–66
After party, 141–142
After to-do list, 175
Air conditioning, 179
Alan, Tim, 78
Alcohol, 52–53
A-line dress, 82
Alternative bridal attire, 103
Animals, 131
Announcement, of engagement, 5–6
Appointments, for dress shopping, 93–96
April, 19–20
Attire
    alternative, 103
    for groom, 104–105
    for wedding party, 133–136

Bachelorette party, 138–140
Bachelor party, 138–140

Baker, 57–61
Ball gown, 83
Band(s) (ring)
    alternatives with, 118–122
    in bracelet, 119
    caring for, 117–118
    on different fingers, 118
    engravings in, 112–113
    exchange of, 168
    gems in, 111–112, 116
    insurance for, 118
    jeweler questions for, 114–115
    matching vs. non-matching, 115
    metal, 109–110
    as necklace, 119
    piercings instead of, 119–120
    researching, 108–113
    shopping for, 108, 113–116
    stones in, 111–112, 116
    stories, 120–122

sustainability and, 116
tattoos instead of, 119–120
time to purchase, 106–107
Band (music), 62–64
Bar style, for stones in
    wedding band, 111
Bartender, 52–53
Barware, 76
Best man, 130, 182–183
Beverages, 52–53
Birdcage veil, 88
Blusher veil, 88
Body type, 81
Borrowed items, 102
Boss, on guess list, 147–148
Bouquet, 68
Boxes, for organization, 17
Boyfriend. See Groom
Bra, for dress shopping, 95
Bridal shower, 136–138
Bridesmaids. See Wedding
    party(ies)
Bronte, Emily, 1
Brosious, Sara, 80
Brunch, 142–143
Brush train, 87
Budget. See also Cost
    average costs and, 24
    dress, 101–103
    musts, 27–28

organization and, 28–30
payers in, 23–24
in planning, 18
priorities in, 25–28
for wedding party, 133
Bustles, in dress, 86

Cake baker, 57–61
Cascade bouquet, 68
Cash bar, 53
Cassell, Katherine, 29, 39,
    41, 46
Caterer, 50–57
Cathedral veil, 89
Ceremony, 185–186
    orchestrating, 164–169
    pre-, 183–185
    space, 36–38
    time between, and
        reception, 42
    transportation from, to
        reception, 72–73
    transportation to, 72
    vows and, 164–169
Chairs, 76
Channel style, for stones in
    wedding band, 111
Chapel train, 88
Chapel veil, 89
Children, 146

Cleaning, of ring, 117–118
Clothing. *See* Attire; Dress
Color, of dress, 91
Column dress, 83
Cost. *See also* Budget
  average, 24
  breakdown, 25
Courses, of food, 51
Court train, 87

Date, in planning, 18–21
Day before, 179–181
Days of week, 20
Daytime wedding, 20
Declaration of intent, 168
Decorations, 69–71
Designer, for invitations,
  150–152
Diamond mining, 116
Dinnerware, 76
Division of labor, 12–14
DJ, 62–64
Draping, in skirt, 86
Dress
  A-line, 82
  alternatives to, 103
  body type and, 81
  budget-conscious, 101–103
  choice of, 78–79
  color, 91

column, 83
empire, 83
first steps for, 79–80
fit and flare, 83
length, 84
making your own, 103
mermaid, 82
mini, 82
movement test for, 97
neckline of, 84–85
princess, 83
purchase, 99–101
religion and, 84
shopping, 22, 92–101
silhouette, 82–84
size, 100
skirt of, 85–86
sleeves on, 91
style, 81–87
trying on, 96–99
venue and, 80
weight and, 81
Drinks, 52–53

Elastic loop veil base, 89
Elbow veil, 88
Email account, 21
Embellishments, of veil, 90
Empire dress, 83
End of night, 190

Engagement
    announcement, 5–6
    enjoying, 2
    families and, 7–8
    gifts, 11–12
    informing others of, 2–6
    jealousy over, 6–7
    parents and, 7–8
    party, 9–12
    photos, 5–6
    questions about, 8–9
Engagement ring, 108, 110, 119
Engravings, in wedding band,
    112–113
Entertainment, 22, 62–66
Expenses, 24
Extended family, 146

Families
    engagement and, 7–8
    extended, 146
    food and, 61
    gifts for, 163–164
    guest list requests and, 147
Family heirlooms, 102
Favors, 22, 160–164
Fiancé. See Groom
Finances. See Budget; Cost
Fingertip veil, 88
Finnamore, Suzanne, 144

Fireworks, 66
Fit-and-flare, 83
Flounce, in dress, 86
Flower girls, 130–131,
    135–136, 163
Flowers, 66–69
Flyaway veil, 88
Food
    cake, 57–61
    caterer for, 50–57
    courses, 51
    family and, 61
    friends and, 61
    menu planning, 54–56

Games, 65
Gems, in wedding band,
    111–112, 116
Gift baskets, 161–162
Gift registry, 154–157
Gifts
    engagement, 11–12
    for major players, 162–164
    shower, 139
Gloves, 92
Gold wedding bands, 109
Groom
    attire for, 104–105
    division of labor with, 12–14
    in dress shopping, 92

Groomsmen, 105. *See also* Wedding party(ies)
Guaranteed NOs, 146
Guest list, 22, 32, 145–148
Guignet, Jolene, 56–57
Gypsy style, for stones in wedding band, 111

Hair, 169–171
Hair accessories, for dress shopping, 95
Halter neckline, 85
Hand-tied bouquet, 68
Heat, 179
Heirlooms, 102
Honeymoon, 171–174
Husband. *See* Groom
Hydration, 184

Infinity style, for stones in wedding band, 111
Insurance, 39, 118
Interactive display, 65
Invitations
    designers for, 150–152
    information on, 148–150
    organization with, 153–154
    verbal, 147
Invocation, 167

Jacket, 92
Jealousy, 6–7

Keen, Sam, 123
Koss, Phyllis, 43

Length, of dress, 84
Lewis, C. S., 106
License, marriage, 178–179
Lists, in planning, 17–18
Look book, for dress shopping, 95

Maid of honor, 130, 181–182
Makeup, 169–171, 185
Makeup artist, 170
Mantilla veil, 89
Marriage license, 178–179
Matron of honor, 130
Menu planning, 54–56
Mermaid dress, 82
Metal wedding bands, 109–110
Microdermal piercings, 120
Mini dress, 82
Moms, 135–136
Month, in date setting, 19, 20
Mothers, 135–136
Movement test, for dress shopping, 97
Music, 62–64

Nail artist, 170
Neckline, of dress, 84–85
Night before, 181
Nighttime wedding, 20
Nosegay, 68

O'Connell, Mark, 46
Officiant, 37–38
Open bar, 53
Organization
    boxes for, 17
    budget and, 28–30
    with invitations, 153–154
    lists for, 17–18
    space for, 16–18
OurWeddingDay.com, 6

Palladium wedding bands, 109
Panty hose, for dress
    shopping, 95
Papritz, Carew, 15
Parents, engagement and, 7–8
Parking, 74–75
Parties, 136–143. *See also*
    Reception; Wedding
    party(ies)
Partner
    division of labor with, 12–14
    in dress shopping, 92
Party, engagement, 9–12

Payers, 23–24
Performances
    (entertainment), 66
Petals, in dress, 85
Pets, 131
Photo booth, 65
Photographer, 47–50
Photos
    engagement, 5–6
    pre-wedding, 183
    wedding, 188
Photo slideshow, 65
Piercings, 119–120
Planning
    budget in, 18
    date in, 18–21
    lists for, 17–18
    preparing for, 15–16
    religion in, 21
    space for, 16–18
Platinum wedding bands, 109
Pleats, in dress, 86
Plus ones, 145
Pomander, 68
Pregnancy, 91, 129
Princess dress, 83
Priorities, 25–28
Processional, 167
Programs, 152–153
Pronouncement, 168

Reception, 188–190
  entertainment at, 22, 62–66
  site features, 40–41
  site for, 38–42
  time between, and
    ceremony, 42
  transportation from, 73
  transportation to, from
    ceremony, 72–73
Recessional, 168–169
Registry, gift, 154–157
Rehearsal dinner, 141
Religion, 21, 84
Rental agencies, 75–77
Rented clothing, 102
Ring(s)
  alternatives with, 118–122
  in bracelet, 119
  caring for, 117–118
  on different fingers, 118
  engagement, 108, 110, 119
  engravings in, 112–113
  exchange of, 168
  gems in, 111–112, 116
  insurance for, 118
  jeweler questions for,
    114–115
  matching vs. non-
    matching, 115
  metal, 109–110

  as necklace, 119
  piercings instead of, 119–120
  researching, 108–113
  shopping for, 108, 113–116
  stones in, 111–112, 116
  stories, 120–122
  sustainability and, 116
  tattoos instead of, 119–120
  time to purchase, 106–107
Ring bearers, 130–131,
  135–136, 163
Round bouquet, 68
Royal train, 88

Sample sales, 102
Save the Date, 148
Scoop neckline, 85
Season, in date choice, 20
Seating charts, 157–159
Semi-cathedral train, 88
Shishak, Lei, 59
Shoes, for dress shopping, 95
Shopping
  for dress, 22, 79–80,
    92–101
  for rings, 108, 113–116
Silhouettes, dress, 82–84
Size
  dress, 100
  venue, 32

Skirt, of dress, 85–86
Sleeves, of dress, 91
Slideshow, 65
Smoking, 184–185
Social media, 2–3
Space, for planning, 16–18.
　　See also Venue(s)
Square neckline, 85
Stones, in wedding band,
　　111–112, 116
Strapless neckline, 85
Streamers, in dress, 85
Style, 22
　　dress, 81–87
　　venue and, 32–35
Stylist, 170
Summer, 20
Sustainability, weddings rings
　　and, 116
Sweetheart neckline, 85

Tables, 76
Tails, in dress, 86
Tattoos, 119–120
Tax day, 19–20
Team, for dress shopping, 93
Temperature, 179
TheKnot.com, 6
Theme, 22
Thoreau, Henry David, 176

Tiers, in dress, 85
Titanium wedding bands, 109
Toasts, 189
To-do list, after, 175
Tossing bouquet, 69
Train, 86–88
Transportation, 72–75
Trying on dresses, 96–99

Veil, 86, 87, 88–90
Vendors
　　gifts for, 164
　　order of booking for,
　　　43–44
　　questions for, 45–47
　　researching, 44
Venue(s)
　　ceremony, 36–38
　　date and, 19
　　dress and, 80
　　guest list and, 32
　　reception, 38–42
　　rehearsal dinner, 141
　　research on, 31
　　size, 32
　　style and, 32–35
Verbal invites, 147
Videographer, 49–50
V-neck, 85
Vows, 164–169

Waltz veil, 89
Watteau train, 87
Wedding day, 183–190
Wedding dress. *See* Dress
Wedding-in-a-box, 41
Wedding party(ies), 22
    animals in, 131
    asking, 127–129
    attire, 133–136
    bonding in, 132–133
    emotions with, 126–127
    gifts for, 162–164
    mixed, 128

    opinions from, 126–127
    pregnancy in, 129
    seating of, 159
    selection of, 124–136
    symmetry with, 124
    traits of, 125–128
Wedding planner, 29–30, 164
Wedding programs, 152–153
Week before, 176–179
Weight, 81
Weiss, Mindy, 117
Wire comb veil base, 89
Work friends, 146

"True love stories never have endings."
—RICHARD BACH

"A happy marriage is a long conversation which
always seems too short."
—ANDRE MAUROIS